Betrayal & Beyond

LEADER'S GUIDE

FASHIONING A COURAGEOUS HEART

Diane Roberts and Shari Chinchen

BETRAYAL & BEYOND LEADER'S GUIDE

By Diane Roberts and Shari Chinchen

Other contributing writers:
Ted Roberts
Jane Carter
Teri Vietti
Elizabeth Drago

Published by
Pure Desire Ministries International
719 NE Roberts Avenue, Gresham, OR 97030
www.puredesire.org | 503.489.0230
ISBN 978-1-943291-01-4

The stories presented of individual lives in this leader's guide are true and accurate. The details have been adjusted to prevent personal identification. In some cases the story presented is a compilation of the histories of several individuals. The compilation, however, doesn't affect the clinical or theological veracity of the stories.

TABLE OF CONTENTS

WELCOME

Thank you for partnering with Pure Desire to invest in and support those whose lives have been shattered by the impact of betrayal and broken trust. Before you commit to leading a Betrayal & Beyond group, let us give you a "job description" of sorts. As a group leader, your goal is to finish well, not perfect, but well—and not just finish by yourself. Your objective should include the intention to influence others so they can join you and reach their fullest potential as they travel with you on your journey of healing.

David is a great example of a leader who, with all his imperfections, was called a man after God's own heart. He is listed as one of the heroes of the faith in Hebrews 11. He is called a man who served his generation in Acts 13:36. As a Pure Desire group leader, you, like David, are a warrior who has fought this battle yourself and are now serving your generation of women who are also entering this battle. You are God's instrument, not only moving into new levels of personal healing, but also inspiring, encouraging, affirming, believing in, and serving the members in your group. At times, you are creating and developing a vision for your group, giving opportunity for the members to buy in and take ownership of the hope and freedom available through Jesus as presented in the Betrayal & Beyond materials.

Because you too, as a leader, continue to move toward health and healing, you have a unique opportunity to learn to live vulnerably and authentically in view of your group. When you experience ongoing personal growth, your group has the privilege of participating in your success. They may experience hope for the first time.

Additionally, when you have a bad week, your group has the opportunity to experience a healthy response to challenges. When failure and difficulty happens (and it will; we all fail), you will have the opportunity to embrace the pain or hide the truth. Remember, your behavior does not define you, only your salvation through Christ does. When you choose to be vulnerable and transparent with your failures, you demonstrate courage.

> Great leaders inspire. They maintain a hopeful attitude, even in the face of discouraging setbacks, constant criticism and abundant opposition. People don't follow discouraged leaders. They follow those who persist with hope.[1]
>
> RICK WARREN

---

1. Rick Warren, *Ladies' Home Journal,* Oct. 2008

INTRODUCTION

For 25 years, the Lord has led Pure Desire in a ministry of support, healing, and restoration. Through the development of curriculum—uniquely designed to provide a theologically and clinically proven process—and training conferences, the message of grace and freedom is becoming visible in small groups all over the country.

Families are experiencing change from negative family systems that have dominated for generations. Pure Desire groups, led by courageous lay leaders in the church, are answering the call of the wounded and offering a safe place where vulnerability is appearing for the first time in many lives.

With the explosion in brain research, it is now possible to understand the devastating effects of technology on our culture. Pure Desire groups offer continuing education, resources, and the training necessary to protect our families from sexual addiction and the unhealthy sexual messages that permeate our culture and bombard us everywhere we turn.

God has called Pure Desire to help local churches, and their frequently overloaded pastors, address the unspoken truth of sexual addiction within society and the church community. Through a full assortment of resource materials, clinical treatment options, partnership opportunities, and conference presentations, Pure Desire is positioned as a leader in providing Christ-centered recovery options for those ensnared in sexual addiction, as well as those suffering in the wake of their spouse's secret sin.

Teens and young adults, both male and female, are the #1 demographic target of porn producers and entertainment media. For that reason, Pure Desire offers resource material and groups to support this critically-important population, as well, who are often overlooked and go unnoticed in the battle for healthy sexuality.

Pure Desire programs and resources address the evidence-based understanding that sexual bondage and the associated struggles are a family systems issue, not just an individual problem. Wives who suddenly discover their husbands have been living a secret life, desperately need a ministry to support them, so they can experience healing and the marriage can be restored. Our approach to care is practical and applicable to daily life and offers an array of resources to guide Christ's ministry for men, women, and youth, which can be found at puredesire.org.

BETRAYAL & BEYOND WORKBOOK

How did he get this way? How can I tell if he is getting better? Can I ever trust him again? What do I do now? The *Betrayal & Beyond Workbook* was designed to answer these questions and more. Created to be experienced in a group setting, this resource provides valuable tools, biblical wisdom, and testimonies by courageous women who found hope, help, and encouragement through their personal journey.

BETRAYAL & BEYOND JOURNAL

The *Betrayal & Beyond Journal* is a companion resource that promotes the daily commitment to self-care and health. It provides tools vital to one's healing and reinforces the importance of facing loss and processing anger and hurt. As you journal through this journey, you will see how God can do beyond what we can even think or dream.

BETRAYAL & BEYOND LEADER'S GUIDE

As a Pure Desire group leader you, too, are moving toward health and healing. However, a group leader desires to inspire encourage, affirm, believe in, and serve the members in her group. The *Betrayal & Beyond Leader's Guide* will help you create and develop a vision for your group, giving opportunity for each member to buy in and take ownership of the hope and freedom available through Jesus.

BETRAYAL & BEYOND KIT

The Betrayal & Beyond Kit includes a copy of the *Betrayal & Beyond Workbook*, *Journal*, and *Peace Beyond the Tears*. It is available at a reduced cost.

HOW THIS LEADER'S GUIDE IS ORGANIZED

The *Betrayal & Beyond Workbook* is divided into nine chapters; each chapter consists of four or five lessons. This guide will walk you through each lesson and help you prepare to successfully lead your group.

FOR EACH LESSON,

THE LEADER WILL NEED:	THE GROUP MEMBER WILL NEED:
• *Betrayal & Beyond Leader's Guide* • *Betrayal & Beyond Workbook* • *Betrayal & Beyond Journal*	• *Betrayal & Beyond Workbook* • *Betrayal & Beyond Journal*

THE *BETRAYAL & BEYOND LEADER'S GUIDE* INCLUDES:

❶ **Group Leader Description/Qualifications**

❷ **Before Launching Your Group**

❸ **Betrayal & Beyond Overview**

❹ **Group Tools**

❺ **Group Structure 40/60/20**
- Individual Review—40 minutes
- Lesson Review/Homework—60 minutes
- Summary—20 minutes
- Overview of a Typical Group Meeting

❻ **Group Orientation**
- Suggested Lesson Plan
- Main Activity for Orientation
- Betrayal & Beyond Survey (Optional)
- Betrayal & Beyond Questionnaire (Optional)
- Brain Bender Activity (Optional)

❼ **Pre-Group Leader Prep**
- Primary focus for each lesson
- Recommended chapter reading/viewing
- Overview for each chapter and lesson

❽ **Frequently Asked Questions**

❾ **Appendix**
- Integrating New Women
- Betrayal & Beyond Survey
- Betrayal & Beyond Questionnaire
- Recommended Reading
- What a Polygraph Test Can and Cannot Do
- PTSI Analysis Overview
- Sample Betrayal & Beyond Letter
- Wife's Inventory for Disclosure
- The Karpman Triangle Exercise

The apostle Paul didn't care much for the applause of others, but he did care deeply for the smile of the Lord. He knew that "without faith it is impossible to please God, because anyone who comes to him must believe that he exists and that he rewards those who earnestly seek him." (Hebrews 11:6 NIV).

Dr. Elton Trueblood said, "Faith is not belief without proof, but trust without reservation."[2] As a group leader you will experience regular opportunity to trust the Lord. Leading a Pure Desire group is not an easy undertaking. There may be a day when you have to tell your group that you don't know the answer to a question or you may have to ask a group member to leave your group. You will experience challenging exercises, as well as difficult questions and trauma stories.

We know that Paul had many struggles as a leader and regularly wrestled with sin. He didn't always agree with those he was serving with, he experienced opposition when he communicated the truth, and he endure a great deal of persecution. Yet, he was a man passionately consumed with trusting the Lord no matter what he faced. That was his driving ambition. He was that kind of leader. He had the highest goal, expressed the widest devotion, and was driven by the deepest motive.

> WITHOUT GOALS, AND PLANS TO REACH THEM, YOU ARE LIKE A SHIP THAT HAS SET SAIL WITH NO DESTINATION.[3]
> FITZHUGH DODSON

A primary calling upon Pure Desire is to raise up leaders to advance the message of restoration and healing in the church. We partner with men and women who understand the harmful impact of sexual addiction and desire to take back spiritual territory the enemy sought to destroy. To be well equipped to lead a Betrayal & Beyond group, we recommend the following:

ATTEND LEADERSHIP TRAINING

The Pure Desire University was created to equip the church with an understanding of the factors that create and reinforce addictive sexual behavior. It provides a comprehensive understanding of not only sex addiction, but the understanding and tools required to lead a group that offers hope and health to women.

Upon completion of the leadership training conference, participants will demonstrate the following:

- Understanding of the role shame plays in the addiction process
- Recognition of the significance of God's continued and persistent grace in the lives of the addicted, which provides a foundational tool for restoration and healing

2. D. Elton Trueblood. BrainyQuote.com, Xplore Inc, 2016. http://www.brainyquote.com/quotes/quotes/d/deltontru130096.html, accessed April 8, 2016.
3. Fitzhugh Dodson. Very Best Quotes. http://www.verybestquotes.com/goals-goal-setting-quotes-inspirational-quotes-about-goals/, accessed April 8, 2016.

- Knowledge of the truth behind the neurochemistry of addiction, from both a biological and biblical perspective
- Realization of how childhood trauma and woundedness perpetuates addictive behavior
- Identification of the specific behavioral triggers that contribute to addiction
- Development of an understanding of the many Pure Desire resources available for individuals, groups, or families, and the practical application of each product

VIEW THE CONQUER SERIES

The *Conquer Series: A Battle Plan for Purity*, unrivaled in its scope and authority, is a cinematic teaching series that offers men proven principles and practical tools to break free from pornography. The five-week curriculum is hosted by Dr. Ted Roberts, a former Marine fighter pilot who has, for 30+ years, helped thousands of men find freedom and walk in purity. Women's group leaders will glean helpful information from this series. It will give them an overview of many of the concepts, especially those refer red to in Chapters 2 and 4 in regards to the brain and trauma.

HEALTH AND ACCOUNTABILITY

It is best if group leaders have participated in a Betrayal & Beyond group previously, have experience using the resources and tools, and understand key elements of group dynamics. In addition, it is important to have accountability with your church leadership, regularly meeting with an accountability contact—of the same gender—that is not currently working through personal betrayal issues. We also recommend that you have an active Safety Plan that supports healthy boundaries with a focus on personal growth and be personally implementing and actively using the tools you have acquired from Betrayal & Beyond. Having ongoing, scheduled meetings with your accountability contact to talk about the progress of group members (keeping their names anonymous), as well as your own active Safety Plan and personal progress, will provide a strong foundation for your group.

CHURCH SUPPORT

If you are aligned with a church, seek out appropriate pastoral covering. Your church leadership can help you advertise your group and can help women who are seeking health find you. Coordinate with your church's Seven Pillars of Freedom group for men: The wives of the men in these groups need to be offered support through the Betrayal & Beyond curriculum.

If you are not aligned with a church body, or if your church is not yet ready to accept the need for your group, pray earnestly for such covering.

PRAYER SUPPORT

Invite friends or women in your church to provide ongoing prayer support as you lead; for the women who will attend; and for their healing, families, and marriages. *Remember: Guard the confidentiality of the group, no names or specific situations may be shared with prayer partners.*

DETERMINE YOUR CLASS SCHEDULE

Consistency is important: Plan to meet at the same day and time every week. A two hour class is highly recommended. The ideal group size is four to six women; plan to break into smaller groups if you have more than six women attending.

Other things to consider:

- Will you begin a new chapter at the beginning of each month?
- If so, what will you do during months that have a 5th meeting day?
- What about holidays and vacations?

ADVERTISE YOUR GROUP

Promote your group in as many ways as possible: Church bulletins, fliers, social media, word of mouth. Contact Pure Desire to have your group placed on our website's group locator. Be sure to include a way for women to contact you (phone, text, or email) with any questions prior to the orientation session.

DEVELOP A CO-LEADER

Carrying the burden of leadership all by yourself is challenging. You need someone to come alongside you, to share this journey. Seek out a co-leader to assist you.

NETWORK WITH OTHER LEADERS

Group leadership can often feel lonely. Collaborating with other group leaders can help you feel more supported. Other group leaders can share insights on issues they have encountered in their groups, help with specific questions, and offer additional prayer support. Contact Pure Desire (503.489.0230 or puredesire.org) to be introduced to your Pure Desire Regional Groups Leader.

··

INTEGRATE NEW WOMEN INTO YOUR GROUP

New women may join at the beginning of any chapters between Chapter 1 and Chapter 7. However, we highly recommend that women complete an orientation session before joining an existing group. This orientation may include several women or may be one-on-one with a leader.

Beyond the lessons in Chapter 1, it is not necessary for a woman to "catch up" by completing missed chapters to bring her current to the existing group. She will want to do those lessons she missed as part of her healing, but should complete them during another group cycle.

··

REGIONAL GROUP LEADERS

Pure Desire's approach to ministry requires trusted leaders that are reliable and represent Pure Desire's values and practices. Our leaders serve in one or more of three areas: Event Speakers, Regional Group Leaders, and Group Leaders.

A Regional Group Leader (RGL) trains, develops, and supports volunteer Group Leaders in their region. RGLs demonstrate and administer Pure Desire Group Best Practices and standards within the organization's policies and procedures. They provide the leadership, innovation, and stability necessary for consistent improvement, while ensuring a positive and gracious approach to Pure Desire groups. To find the RGL for your area, visit puredesire.org/groups/rgls.

Betrayal & Beyond is designed to help bring healing to women who have experienced betrayal and broken trust through their spouse's sexual addiction. God desires to bring restoration and lay a new foundation of healing and grace. The following gives you an overview of the skills that are taught over the course of the curriculum.

Managing the Crisis is composed of Chapters 1-3, and each chapter consists of four lessons. During this section of the resource, women come to understand the characteristics of sexual addiction, how to break through denial, grasp the basic components that are needed to begin to rebuild trust in a recovering addict, and identify the different realities that women and men experience in this type of crisis. As each chapter develops, group members will understand the cycle of addiction, explore the relationship between trauma and addiction, and identify the basic signs of recovery in an addict. As women transition to Chapter 3, they begin to grasp that their own brokenness has affected their marriage. They learn about the Karpman Triangle,[4] begin to identify personal issues that need restoration, and understand the difference between survival and projected lies. Projected lies are when others take their own fears and hurts and project them onto someone else. Survival lies are the lies you tell yourself as a way to survive.

My Healing Journey includes Chapters 4-6, with four to five lessons in each chapter. During these chapters, group members begin to look more deeply at how personal trauma has affected them and identify coping mechanisms and patterns. They are able to recognize personal codependent behaviors and the difference between self-care and self-centeredness. Women learn how to use the FASTER Scale[5] for self-awareness, healing, and reducing anxiety. They begin to see the difference between healthy/safe and unhealthy/unsafe relationships, and experience the personal power of choosing vulnerability and proximity with others.

The Courageous Road to Restoration is Chapters 7-9. Each chapter contains four lessons. By this time, group members are ready to understand the issues surrounding repressed anger, come to grips with the power of real and perceived losses, and grasp the reality of how betrayal has affected their life. They are able to understand the concept of true forgiveness and recognize the effect of past trauma on their ability to forgive. Finally, women are able to identify and pursue next, healthy steps for healing and growth and commit to maintain a healthy support system.

Note: Chapters 1-3 are difficult because most women are in shock and are facing the reality of what their husband's sexual activity has been. Chapters 4-6 are sometimes equally or more difficult because now they are facing issues in their own life that they have dismissed or were unaware of for years. Using their copies of the *Betrayal & Beyond Journal* will help them begin to process their own past and pain. In Chapters 7-9 women will be given tools to face and release their own past trauma and pain.

---

4. Stephen Karpman, M.D., "Overlapping Egograms," Transactional Analysis Journal 4, No 4 (October 1974) 16-19.
5. Michael Dye, *The Genesis Process* (Auburn, CA: Michael Dye, 2006) www.genesisprocess.org.

CHAPTER OBJECTIVES

CHAPTER ONE: WHERE DO I START?
- Understand the characteristics of sexual addiction
- Break through delusion
- Grasp basic components needed for trust in a recovering addict
- Identify different realities for women and men in crisis

CHAPTER TWO: UNDERSTANDING THE NATURE OF ADDICTION
- Understand the cycle of addiction
- Grasp the concept of co-morbidity
- See the relationship between trauma and addiction
- Identify the basic signs of recovery in an addict

CHAPTER THREE: COMMITMENT TO PERSONAL HEALING
- Understand what disclosure looks like for the wife and family members
- Grasp the idea that her brokenness affects their marriage
- Understand the basic roles of the Karpman Triangle
- Identify personal issues that need restoration
- Know the difference between survival and projected lies
- See how past beliefs drive men and women to dysfunction, away from taking care of themselves
- Consider temporary diminishing/ending of ministry or other roles to focus on personal healing

CHAPTER FOUR: TRAUMA'S UNDERCURRENT
- Identify how trauma has personally affected them
- Note patterns and cycles identified on a personal timeline

CHAPTER FIVE: UNTANGLING UNHEALTHY RELATIONSHIPS
- Identify codependency in her life
- Identify the difference between self-care and self-centeredness
- Know her personal coping mechanisms and patterns
- Understand how to use the FASTER Scale and Double Bind for self-awareness, healing, and reducing anxiety

CHAPTER SIX: HEALTHY BOUNDARIES
- See the difference between real and perceived losses
- Understand the issues around repressed anger
- Express the reality of how betrayal has affected her life

CHAPTER SEVEN: FACING MY GRIEF AND ANGER
- Understand the power of real and perceived losses and the grieving process
- Express the reality of how betrayal has affected her life

CHAPTER EIGHT: HEALING AND FORGIVENESS
- Understand the concept of true forgiveness
- Recognize the effect of past trauma on the ability to forgive

CHAPTER NINE: RESTORING HEALTH AND CLOSENESS
- Gain the ability to identify and pursue next healthy steps for healing and growth
- Maintain a healthy support system

GROUP GUIDELINES

Betrayal & Beyond Workbook, Page 289: Pure Desire recommends the following Group Guidelines. Read through the guidelines and ask each group member if they agree to them. Discuss whether your group would like to create additional guidelines. Post them during each group meeting; this provides a reminder and clarifies the expectations for the group, as well as each individual. Review the guidelines when a new member joins your group and at the beginning of each new chapter.

Confidentiality is Essential	What is said in the group is not shared outside the group.
Self-focus	Speak only for yourself and avoid giving advice.
Limit Sharing	Give everyone a chance to share.
Respect Others	Let everyone find her own answers.
Regular Attendance	Let your leader or co-leader know if you can't attend a meeting.
Start and End on Time	Make it a priority to begin and end your group on time.
Homework Completion	Review each lesson and take time to complete your assignments.
Responsibility	If you feel uncomfortable with anything happening in the group or among group members, share your concern with the group or with the leader or co-leader.

MEMO OF UNDERSTANDING

Betrayal & Beyond Workbook, Page 288: In order to experience deep and lasting healing and restoration after betrayal, you need to be a member of a Pure Desire group. Your Betrayal & Beyond group will consist of women who are in overwhelming situations. To be sure, they are really struggling. But, you will learn to love these women, celebrate with them, and value this group. These are the women who will stand in each other's corner, be on their knees for one another, and love their group members in the midst of each other's healing journey.

After reading through the Group Guidelines with your group, read through the Memo of Understanding. State the importance of confidentiality within the group. This tool defines and communicates what confidentiality is and forewarns group members that if confidentiality is violated, they will be asked to leave the group. Also make clear the circumstances that might cause a leader to break confidentiality.

In addition, a signed Memo of Understanding allows you—as a group leader—to break confidentiality if you believe someone's life or health is at risk.

BETRAYAL & BEYOND SURVEY

Page 66: If you have a group that has more than six members, use the survey to help you determine which small group to place members in. Consider placing at least two women with similar situations or issues in the same group. This provides an opportunity for them to feel less alone in their circumstance. Let the women know that the information they share on the survey is confidential and will be shredded at the end of the group meeting.

BETRAYAL & BEYOND QUESTIONNAIRE

Page 67: The anonymous questionnaire includes five questions. The answers to these questions should be shared with the small group leaders so they can serve the group more effectively.

FASTER SCALE

***Betrayal & Beyond Workbook*, Page 154:** The FASTER Scale for preventing relapse came as a result of searching for an answer to the following question from Romans 7: Why do we repeat behaviors that are destructive and sinful?

Many addicts try so hard to change and are motivated by the devastating consequences of their addictions, yet still relapse. The FASTER Scale is the result of the effort to unravel the mystery of relapse. This tool has proven to be very accurate in predicting and preventing relapse by identifying and intervening in pre-relapse behavior patterns.

DOUBLE BIND

***Betrayal & Beyond Workbook*, Page 157:** The Double Bind is a tool for healing through understanding what your addictive behaviors are there for and what they are protecting you from.[6] All destructive coping behaviors involve a Double Bind. Consciously or subconsciously, you are in a lose/lose situation. Making your choices consciously and taking steps of faith to move past where "the rubber meets the road" to a place of real recovery and healing take place.[7] For example, if I take the risk and expose my secrets (trusting others), they will reject me or gossip. If I don't ask for help, I will stay stuck and isolated. Staying stuck in the middle of a lose/lose situation produces feelings of anger, frustration, hopelessness, depression, anxiety, and fear. These are the very emotions that coping behaviors anesthetize. Resolving Double Binds is the key for change.[8]

6. Michael Dye, *The Genesis Process* (Auburn, CA: Michael Dye, 2006) 233.
7. Ibid. 269.
8. Ibid. 57.

SAFETY PLAN FOR MARRIED WOMEN

***Betrayal & Beyond Workbook*, Page 177:** Many women, after discovering their husband's activity, can go from one extreme to the other: overfunctioning or underfunctioning. Each of these responses usually comes as a result of fear and feeling overwhelmed by their situation. How do you establish healthy boundaries with the addict? Three questions are important for you to ask yourself:

1. What is the desired outcome I seek?
2. For whom is the boundary intended?
3. Am I protecting myself or trying to change the addict?

This plan consists of the steps that represent personal healing, increasing your trust in your spouse (if you're in relationship with him), and preparing in advance for the possibility of his sexual addiction relapse. Although you do not have control over your spouse's addiction and healing, you do have a choice about how to respond to him, what you want your own healing to look like, and how to provide protection for yourself and your children.

SAFETY PLAN FOR SINGLE WOMEN

***Betrayal & Beyond Workbook*, Page 294:** A large part of caring for yourself is setting healthy boundaries. Use this tool to help identify your values and how to communicate them to others. Identify your sexual limits before dating and ask a potential boyfriend about his beliefs. If you are in a committed dating situation, share your beliefs and values with him, and share your commitment to purity—whether it is a recommitment or an original commitment—with a trusted friend.

COUPLE'S SAFETY PLAN

***Betrayal & Beyond Workbook*, Page 300:** As women finish the material in Chapter 9, they will be encouraged to work with their spouse to come up with a Couple's Safety Plan together. Through their Pure Desire group journey, they have gained important individual tools for a new lifestyle of healing. The Couple's Safety Plan gives them an opportunity to combine and add to the tools they want to incorporate into their life as a couple. Only through new habits as individuals and as a couple will lasting change take place.

DEVELOPING INTIMACY EXERCISE

***Betrayal & Beyond Workbook*, Page 298:** God has a great life planned ahead for you, as a couple, that includes a life of authentic intimacy. Clinical studies reveal that the ability to talk openly and honestly about our desires, fantasies, and sex life with your spouse contributes to a more fulfilling relationship in marriage.

How do we get past what is awkward or uncomfortable and learn to communicate our sexual preferences? Every great love story starts with a great script. Use this tool to create your own script by completing this exercise with your spouse.

THREE CIRCLES EXERCISE

***Betrayal & Beyond Workbook*, Page 280:** Essentially, the purpose of the Three Circles Exercise is to present the FASTER Scale in a more user-friendly way. It allows women to see what they are working on at a glance. The Three Circles Exercise helps women recognize the codependent rescuing and control issues in their inner circle. Looking at their FASTER Scale will reveal the middle circle behaviors that cause them to fall back into the inner circle. To avoid these two circles, women should identify outer circle behaviors—healthy self-care and healing steps that will help them continue in their healing process. As women heal, their old middle circle behaviors should move to the inner circle and there should be an increased focus on healthy outer-circle behaviors.

POLYGRAPH

***Betrayal & Beyond Workbook*, Page 296:** The polygraph allows an addict's behavior to be measured objectively. It can be used to begin restoring trust in a relationship and can be given within 30 days of disclosure. Additionally, subsequent polygraphs can be given every 90 days to ensure greater accountability. A polygraph cannot guarantee that an addict will not lie again or that they will stop their addictive behavior, but it can promote safety and trust, which leads to a growing intimacy in the relationship. We recommend contacting a Pure Desire CSAT (Certified Sexual Addiction Therapist) if a group member needs help preparing for a polygraph.

FACES EVALUATION

***Betrayal & Beyond Workbook*, Page 73:** Our relationships with our parents affected us in good and bad ways; the reality is, those effects are still influencing our behaviors. Use this tool to evaluate your family of origin and evaluate your relationship with each of your parents.

PTSI

***Betrayal & Beyond Workbook*, Page 100:** Trauma accumulation, with frequency and/or intensity over time, can affect the neurochemistry of our brain; not only the addict's brain. Our limbic system (or survival brain) remembers experiences that result in reactions of flight (running away), fight (confronting), or freeze (emotional paralysis). This tool allows us to take a look in the "rearview mirror" of our life. This is not a clinical test; however, it identifies if issues from your past are affecting you in the present. Time does not heal all wounds, because our survival brain remembers. "Effective healing and recovery must be experiential. It takes an opposite healing experience from the hurt to change the heart."[9] A clinical explanation for leaders can be found on page 71.

COURAGEOUS COMMITMENT TO CHANGE

***Betrayal & Beyond Journal*, Every Lesson from Chapter 6, Lesson 1 On:** This tool addresses a challenge you will be facing during the week or a behavior you have identified that needs to change.

---

9. Michael Dye, *The Genesis Process for Change Groups, Book One* (Auburn, CA: Michael Dye, 2006) www.genesisprocess.org.

The Courageous Commitment to Change is about something you have identified that will help you move forward in your restoration. Fill out the Courageous Commitment to Change in your group time and evaluate the Double Bind (what you have to give up to make this change.)

GROUP CHECK-IN

***Betrayal & Beyond Journal*, Every Lesson from Chapter 6, Lesson 1 On:** Use the Group Check-in to journal your Double Bind and Courageous Commitment to Change. Log the information from your Betrayal & Beyond lesson that was most applicable to your situation and emotionally impactful, and record what actions you have taken to improve your relationship with your husband and/or other significant relationships during the week.

PERSONAL/PROPHETIC PROMISES

***Betrayal & Beyond Journal*, Every Lesson from Chapter 5, Lesson 5 On:** If you stop and think through your life, you will be able to identify several times where God powerfully met you through His Holy Spirit. It may have been during a time of tragedy, pain, or great rejoicing. In these moments, God was revealing not only His character, but also His view of you. You can take these encounters and pair them with Scripture, creating a God-given, personal vision of who you are in Christ.

THE FEELINGS WHEEL

***Betrayal & Beyond Workbook*, Page 291:** As you begin your healing journey, you may experience feelings that you can't identify, or mood swings that seem uncontrollable. You can use the Feeling Wheel to help you identify your feelings.

PRIMARY, SECONDARY, AND TERTIARY EMOTIONS

***Betrayal & Beyond Workbook*, Page 292:** This chart helps us understand that many of our initial emotions have deeper, underlying feelings. The secondary and tertiary emotions may be the true root feeling and yet be masked by the primary emotion for various reasons. This chart is not an all-inclusive list. However, it may help you better identify your own depth of emotions.

ALPHABETIZED EMOTIONS

***Betrayal & Beyond Workbook*, Page 293:** Identifying root emotions take time. Many primary emotions—fear, joy, surprise, anger, love, and sorrow—actually have deeper levels of feelings underneath that may be broken down to second and even third levels which indicate profound, truer root feelings. Use this tool to specifically identify your root emotions.

GROUP STRUCTURE—40/60/20 FORMAT

INDIVIDUAL REVIEW—40 MINUTES

The first 40 minutes is a time for women to share their *Journal* reflections, their thankfulness exercise (beginning in Chapter 4), and/or their Courageous Challenge/FASTER Scale exercise (beginning in Chapter 6). The purpose of the review is to help the women become more aware of the healing processes that are at work in their lives.

LESSON REVIEW & HOMEWORK DEBRIEF—60 MINUTES

The next 60 minutes are reserved for working through the Betrayal & Beyond lesson, *Journal*, and homework. It is important that the women come to group each week with their homework completed. If their work is not complete, they may not share. If group members have not taken the time to complete their homework, responses during group time reflect the lack of preparation. Never read through the lessons as a group; instead ask them to highlight information that stood out to them and then pick and discuss the questions that you think are most important in light of the individual group members and their needs.

SUMMARY—20 MINUTES

Each group ends with a brief look at the next lesson, highlighting any specific areas that may need extra thought or attention, and prayer. This is also time that the women can make arrangements to contact a minimum of three group members during the upcoming week. The purpose of the contacts is to create supportive relationships among women who understand the healing process, to hold each other each accountable for using the tools being learned and to move away from isolation and toward healthy vulnerability in relationship. Pray at the end. Eventually you may want to ask different group members to pray.

OVERVIEW OF A TYPICAL GROUP MEETING

❶ Group Introduction: Welcome, prayer, and short overview of the lesson's key points.

❷ Review an entry from last week's *Betrayal & Beyond Journal* (a specific response, Thankfulness Exercise, FASTER Scale, and/or Courageous Challenge).

❸ Work through the lesson in the *Betrayal & Beyond Workbook* and *Journal.*

❹ Preview and assign next week's lesson, pray, and schedule your accountability contacts for the week.

SUGGESTED LESSON PLAN

TIME	TOPIC	INFORMATION
30 mins.	• Welcome each woman as she arrives • Name tags • Survey & Questionnaire (*Optional*)— ask women to begin filling these out • Words of welcome, share your story and group overview	• Use name tags for at least the first 3 weeks or if you have someone new join the group.
10 mins.	• Review the Memo of Understanding • Collect signed memos	• Make a copy for each woman to sign and collect those signed copies. Please keep them for the entire time a woman is involved in the group.
10 mins.	• Group Guidelines • Review and discuss • Get agreement	• The suggested guidelines are included in the *Workbook* appendix. Read the guidelines out loud. Allow time for discussion and questions. You may want to add one or two guidelines, perhaps about cell phone use, but be cautious about additions. • Too many group rules can feel overwhelming and rigid. Follow the directions on the guidelines page for using the guidelines during group time.
30-60 mins.	• Collage; create a visual of their situation and share their picture with the group. • *Optional Activity to add if you have time): Brain Benders*	• Gather magazines, glue, scissors, and markers. • Follow directions included in this *Leader's Guide*.

10 mins.	• Pray over the women
	• Assignments for next time:
	  ◦ Read & complete Chapter 1, Lesson 1
	  ◦ Complete *Journal* for Chapter 1, Lesson 1
	• Answer any questions
	• Complete Survey, Questionnaire
		• Collect Memo of Understanding, Survey, and Questionnaire before participants leave.
		• Collect contact information of all participants in case you need to contact them during the week.

End on time!

The orientation—first meeting—is a time to help women feel welcome, communicate they are not alone in the process, and assure them that in your group they can find support from other women who understand. Use this time to explain the curriculum and answer any questions they may have.

Initially, women come to the first Betrayal & Beyond group meeting experiencing shame, depression, and fear. The following suggestions can help reduce the emotional turmoil that will be evident as women walk into the meeting. Walking through the door is the hardest thing they will do; take the opportunity to create a safe environment from the first moment you are together as a group:

Share Your Story—Before launching into logistics, consider sharing your story; this will communicate your transparency and vulnerability.

Group Guidelines—The guidelines are designed to create a safe environment for open and honest conversations during group meetings. Read and discuss the following guidelines as a group, including when anyone new joins the group (*Workbook* appendix, page 289).

Memo of Understanding—The Memo of Understanding indicates that you have read and understand the purpose and parameters of PD groups and the moral and ethical obligations of leaders. We recommend that you keep a copy of each group member's Memo of Understanding and provide your church administrator with a copy as well. The Memo of Understanding is very important because it delineates the circumstances under which confidentiality will be broken. Read through the complete document as a group and have each member sign a copy (*Workbook,* page 288).

Discuss Your Group Schedule—Communicate your group schedule, including any holidays, vacations, and alternate focus days.

Group Size—The ideal group size is four to six women; plan to break into smaller groups if you have more than six women attending. Use the survey information to help you decide placement of the women into groups (see appendix, page 66).

Contact Information—Provide your contact information and the best time to contact you outside of group meetings. Should they contact you or someone else in the group if they cannot come? How should missed lessons be handled? Remember, it is important for the safety of the group that members commit to regular attendance. If they plan to miss three or more meetings, this may not be the right time for them to participate.

Exchange Contact Information—During one of the first few meetings, provide an opportunity for group members to exchange phone numbers for making calls during the week. Use the space provided in the front of the *Betrayal & Beyond Journal* to record group member's contact information. Not everyone will want to exchange contact information right away; it may take a couple of weeks to develop trust among your group members. However, by the fourth meeting, women should be making contact with at least two other group members per week, outside of group time.

Prayer as part of group time—Begin and/or end each meeting with prayer! Decide how prayer requests will be made.

MAIN ACTIVITY FOR ORIENTATION
CREATE A COLLAGE

Activity: Make a collage that reflects how the group member is feeling about their current situation.

Directions: Cut out pictures and words from the magazines that represent how the group member is feeling and create a collage on the back inside cover of the *Betrayal & Beyond Workbook* that communicates their thoughts and feelings about their situation.

Provide: Magazines, paper, glue, scissors, and markers

Explain the project to the group. Provide enough time and an ample area to work. Consider playing worship music while the group works. When everyone has completed the activity, ask each woman to share the collage with the whole group. Leaders, be prepared to share your collage **first** as an example.

For online groups—One week before your group meets for the first time, create an email that explains the activity, directions, and supplies needed to do the collage. Clarify that time will be set aside during the first group meeting for each member to share their collage with the group.

Note: During the last four lessons in Chapter 9, provide time to have the women create another collage that reflects their feelings and current situation. We have found that when the initial collage from the first class is compared to the second collage created in the last chapter, there is usually an amazing change. This activity helps women realize how much God has been working in the few months they have been meeting.

....

BETRAYAL & BEYOND SURVEY (OPTIONAL)

If you have a group that has more than six members, use the Betrayal & Beyond Survey to help you determine which small group to place members in. Consider placing at least two women with similar situations or issues in the same group. This provides an opportunity for them to feel less alone in their circumstance. Let the women know that the information they share on the survey is confidential and will be shredded at the end of the group meeting.

For online groups—Group members may or may not feel comfortable filling out the survey and emailing it to you.

....

BETRAYAL & BEYOND QUESTIONNAIRE (OPTIONAL)

The anonymous questionnaire includes five questions. The answers to these questions should be shared with the small group leaders so they can serve the group more effectively.

....

BRAIN BENDER ACTIVITY (OPTIONAL)

The goal of this exercise is that group members recognize the importance of group time to their healing process. Even if they are receiving one-on-one counseling, only the group environment and structure can help them realize they are not alone and that many things they are experiencing are normal. The enemy wants each woman to feel as if she is the only one going through this ordeal, and the shame of it will keep her isolated and hopeless.

DIRECTIONS

1. Allow the women two minutes on their own to figure out as many of the puzzles as they can. Give them the answer to the first one so that everyone will get the idea.

2. After two minutes, ask them to partner with at least two or three other women and work together for about three more minutes. They will find that together they can do more problem solving than by themselves.

3. Since most groups will not be able to figure out all the answers, especially in the limited timeframe, go over the answers with them (The answers appear at the end of these directions).

4. Explain the purpose of the exercise.

    A. By yourself, you can solve a few puzzles. With a small group's help you can figure out almost all of them. With the instructor's help you have all the answers.

    B. Some women in the group will have answers that others do not because of where they are presently walking.

    C. As we walk through various lessons, others may have more experience and will then have an opportunity to help those who are not as far along in the process. God puts us into the Body of Christ so we can support and encourage one another.

ANSWERS

1. "W"
2. "a little bit more"
3. "space ship"
4. "do you understand?"
5. "sunny side up"
6. "check up"
7. "in time"
8. "walk on water"
9. "wash before dinner"
10. "crossroads"
11. "bicycle" or "recycle"
12. "between times" or "in between times"
13. "good over evil"
14. "slow down"
15. "too good to be true"
16. "line up"
17. "inside out"
18. "forecast"
19. "hillbilly"
20. "it's in the bag"
21. "open after hours"
22. "elbow"
23. "lean over backwards"
24. "standing in the corner"
25. "growing up too fast"
26. "open door"
27. "parachutes"
28. "mixed nuts"

BRAIN BENDERS

1 U U	2 bit **MORE**	3 SHI P	4 *STAND ?* ――――――― *DO YOU*
5 Y N N U S	6 K C E H C	7 TI n ME	8 WALK H2O
9 W dinner A dinner S dinner H dinner	10 R O ROADS D S	11 CYCLECYCLE	12 time**B** time

13
 	
good
evil
	14
	S
	  L
	   O
	    W
		15
		GOOD
		GOOD
		BB
		TRUE
			16
			E
			N
			I
			L

17 out	18 cast cast cast cast	19 L I L B E	20 *the it's bag*
21 HOURSopen	22 B **OW**	23 lean sdrawkcab	24 s t a nding

25
   G
  N
 I
W
O   FAST
R   FAST
G
	26
	
	DO OR
		27
		
		chutes
		chutes
			28
			
			UTNS

Created by Teri Vietti

PRE-GROUP LEADER PREP

These pages are designed to help you guide the discussion of the *Betrayal & Beyond Workbook* curriculum, allowing for flexibility in meeting the needs of your group while maintaining the integrity of the curriculum. Be aware that each lesson within each chapter builds on the previous lesson; therefore, it is very important that you, as the leader, are knowledgeable about the entire process and how each lesson fits into the theme of the chapter.

In preparation for your weekly group time, think through and plan what questions might be most relevant for discussion. Since the women in your group are expected to complete their lesson prior to group, the focus of your time together is to evaluate and process the information, not read through the lesson.

We recommend that you read the lesson ahead of the meeting time, read and complete the *Betrayal & Beyond Workbook* and *Journal* along with your group, and always preview at least one lesson ahead of where your group is at any given time.

CHAPTER ONE: WHERE DO I START?

During the four lessons included in Chapter 1, group members will be challenged to overcome the shame they feel from their husband's betrayal by sharing their story with the group. They will come to the understanding that sexual addiction is both a moral and a brain problem. Women will gain perspective on the reality of what they are facing with the hope of what God is speaking to them about their future.

LESSON	PRIMARY FOCUS	CONCEPTS & EXERCISES
❶ How Can I Trust Him?	• Understanding sexual addiction • Recognizing healthy behaviors that can start rebuilding trust • Hope for the future	• Steps Toward Building Trust • Identifying fears and hope
❷ Why It's Not My Fault: The Origins of Sexual Addiction	• The Origins of Sexual Addiction and why Sexual Addiction is not the wife's fault • Overcoming their own shame by sharing their story	• Prepare betrayal stories • The Noose of Addiction • Sharing "My Story"
❸ How Can I Tell If He Is Healing? How Can I Trust Him Again?	• The importance of incorporating healthy structures and boundaries to combat the Acting Out/Acting In cycle • Understanding that transforming change takes three to five years, and that healing is a process that must be walked through.	• Share stories • Acting in/Acting out cycle • Structure/Boundaries • Stages of the Healing Process
❹ What Do I Do Now? Where Do I Go From Here?	• Understanding that her husband may have a different reality than she does when disclosure happens • The importance of identifying her own emotional baggage and how it affects her • Taking authority over her home with respect to her husband's addiction	• Differences between his reality and her reality • Identifying the emotional baggage • Concept of Premature Forgiveness • Praying for her husband

RECOMMENDED READING/VIEWING

Peace Beyond the Tears
👤 by Tina Harris
💲 $15.00
🖥 puredesire.org/pbt

Conquer Series DVD #1
👤 by KingdomWorks Studios
💲 $129.95
🖥 puredesire.org/conquer

ⓘ CONSIDER THIS

LESSON ONE

David's story of betrayal is not only meant to help women see that betrayal does engender trauma, but also how trauma is played out through fight, flight, and freeze. Brené Brown sums up the natural responses in the motto: "Don't puff up (fight), don't shrink back (freeze or flight), but stand your sacred ground."[10] The sacred ground we will be helping women to discover is her personal or prophetic promises in Chapters 4-5.

Introduce the concept of the Steps Toward Building Trust (if you talked about it during the orientation, highlight it again). Throughout the *Workbook* we will be reminding the women of this concept, especially as we introduce the Safety Plan in Chapter 6, Lesson 3 and Chapter 9, Lesson 2. Seeing the addict's consistency over time is the one thing that will continue to build trust in her heart.

Recommend to group members that they read the words of anger that they expressed in their *Betrayal & Beyond Journal*. There will be more opportunities to write out their anger, but it is important that they begin to write it out. Don't be surprised by foul language and euphemisms. Eventually, we want them to replace those with accurate descriptions of their feelings (find The Feelings Wheel in the *Workbook* appendix, page 291). Using foul language is a way of avoiding what they are really feeling. Keep that in mind as we continue to go deeper in the healing process. Relationships in your group will be built over time, and you will be able to encourage women to replace the foul language with accurate feeling descriptions.

LESSON TWO

The more you get to know the women in your group, the more you will be able to choose which questions and comments you need to go over during group. This lesson is designed to help women grapple with the fact that his addiction is not their fault. Hearing from other women who have had the same experiences, especially as they address behaviors and signs that the marriage was eroding, and challenging their twisted beliefs about themselves will help them begin to see that they are not alone.

These questions are also designed to help women see that the addict feels so much shame, he will often project the problems onto his wife, to deflect his own guilt.

In the noose of addiction, underline how trauma and family of origin issues play into the addiction. His addiction started before they knew each other and married. His addiction was how he tried to survive his experiences.

LESSON THREE

One of the most useful concepts in this lesson is helping women see and understand the acting in/ acting out concept. Many women knew about their husband's struggle either before marriage or shortly after marriage, but because he was so good at hiding his addiction they thought it had gone

---

10. Brené Brown, Ph.D. *The Gifts of Imperfection* (Center City, MN: Hazelden, 2010).

away. The truth is, if he has never dealt with the trauma that is driving his addiction, it hasn't gone away. He has just learned ways to "white knuckle" (act in) it for awhile. It will consistently resurface (acting out) because a person can only hold down the pain for so long. This is a scary concept. How do the women know if he is really healing or if he is "white knuckling" it? When he is honestly and proactively pursuing his healing, committed to the work he needs to do in his Pure Desire group, the pattern of acting in and acting out begins to disappear. If he is not working hard for his healing, he is planning to relapse. Therefore, encourage them to believe the behavior not the words.

In this lesson, we present a soft introduction to the Safety Plan. The reason we don't formally introduce this plan until Chapter 6, Lesson 3, is that women who have high Trauma Reaction (there have been other intense traumas in their life), will tend to overreact rather than think through appropriate natural consequences. If they don't understand codependency, they can underreact and may not follow through with the consequences they have designated in their Safety Plan. In a later lesson, the group can help one another come up with balanced, non-punitive consequences that fit the relapse. However, if women are facing the possibilities of STDs, because of infidelity, you may need to help them put a plan together individually.

Note: You might need to take them through Chapter 6, Lesson 3 privately (because the rest of the group may not be ready to do a Safety Plan). If there has been infidelity, they may already have a counselor. Their counselor can facilitate and help her share her Safety Plan with her husband.

The possibility of a polygraph is also brought up in this lesson. I have found that only about 20% of the women in a group may want a polygraph. The appendix gives a good description of what the polygraph can and can't do and describes a full disclosure (see appendix, page 69). We recommend that a CSAT or PSAP counselor help the couple with this process. Contact the Pure Desire office or look at the website to find a qualified counselor. Pure Desire offers counseling online and can take a couple through this process. Here are some important things to understand about the polygraph:

- The polygraph can give the wife a baseline of truth and can help the couple establish a new relationship built on trust.

- The husband will need to write out his full sexual history, outside his present marriage, and a CSAT/PSAP counselor can go over it with him before he takes it to the polygrapher.

- They may need to contact the Pure Desire office, so we can help the polygrapher (outside, independent) understand what is needed in this full disclosure. Most polygraphers are used to dealing with criminals—so they may not understand the purpose of the request.

- As directed in the informational page in the appendix on page 69, the wife will need to come up with 4-6 specific yes or no questions that she would like to ask. There are examples given and we encourage her to not ask too many details but rather focus on important issues—such as, "Do I know the person you had sex with?" "Have you ever had sex with another male?" "You said you cut off all contact with the person you had an affair with—is that true?" (Her group and/or counselor can help her with those questions).

- The husband will need to contact a polygraph examiner that understands a full sexual history disclosure. Again, our offices can coach the examiner if need be.

- The results of the polygraph are **NOT** sent to the husband and wife. They are sent to the counselor—this needs to be stated to the examiner right up front. The counselor will go over the results of the polygraph with the couple.

- Ideally, there would be a woman counselor with the wife when the results are shared. She may be so devastated at any new revelation, she may need another woman to immediately process the information.
- After the results are shared, the counselor can help the husband write out an amends letter where he summarizes all the ways he has hurt his wife and apologizes to her. He can get help writing that letter from his counselor who should read it before it is shared in the counseling office.
- It is important that the wife have support from her group as she goes through this process. We don't recommend a polygraph be given if the wife is not in a Betrayal & Beyond group.

Consider taking an entire group meeting to have women read their stories and process them. Or, you might want to do a half one week and the rest the next week. At some point, consider having them share what they have written in their *Betrayal & Beyond Journal*s about their fears of sharing their story.

LESSON FOUR

This lesson has a number of concepts that need to be processed, including:

- The difference between the husband's and wife's realities. The baggage exercise helps her see all that has been dumped on her because of his sexual activity.
- The idea of premature forgiveness. Many women not only forgive immediately, but also give themselves sexually out of fear that he will go someplace else for his needs. These are codependent responses that are sometimes hidden under the guise of "This is the right thing to do as a Christian."

With Pure Desire clients, we often ask for a 30-90 day sexual sobriety in the marriage. This does two things: it helps the wife refrain from codependent behavior and helps the husband face his pain issues without medicating the pain with sex. These are some of the concepts we will develop throughout the material, but it is good for you to help the women begin to see how many of their responses of premature forgiveness and/or sexual responses may be codependent.

Forgiveness can be premature. Often times, the wife doesn't know the whole story and she doesn't fully know what she is forgiving. She may not realize she has been previously betrayed. As we go through the trauma material, that will be made evident. Sometimes, the husband can become the lightening rod for all her anger; this reaction isn't fair to him. For example, she may have been abandoned by her father, betrayed by her high school boyfriend, and then been betrayed by her husband. In this situation, her husband may become a lightening rod for all of those unprocessed betrayals.

It may be difficult for some women to write a prayer for their spouse. Your goal is to help women understand the benefits of this exercise: for example, if they have children, these prayers are for the father of her children. No matter what the condition of her marriage is, these prayers will affect her children as well.

Encourage group members to read from their copies of the *Betrayal & Beyond Journal* during group. This lesson has many important concepts to process out loud this week.

CHAPTER TWO: UNDERSTANDING THE NATURE OF ADDICTION

In Chapter 2, Understanding the Nature of Addiction, the women will learn about addiction's effects on the brain and investigate the relationship between trauma and addiction in her own life. She will also learn how to prepare herself for full disclosure and discuss the concept of generational curses.

LESSON	PRIMARY FOCUS	CONCEPTS & EXERCISES
❶ Understanding Addiction and Healing	• Understanding our need for Grace	• *Journal* exercises surrounding the impact of grace on our life
❷ Understanding the Effect of Addiction on the Brain	• Understanding how the brain works and how addiction affects brain processes • Understanding that sexual addiction is not just a moral problem, but also a brain problem • Trauma/Abuse and sexual addiction • How your history can affect you in the present	• Writing a prayer for yourself • Writing a prayer for your spouse • Investigating
❸ How the Sex Addict's Brain is Hijacked	• Increasing knowledge base about Sexual Addiction and brain processes • The Limbic System • Process addictions vs. substance addictions • Two things addicts must commit to in order to get free from addiction	• Writing a prayer for your husband in light of two commitments to succeed
❹ Understanding Disclosure & Generational Curses	• Understanding the Full Disclosure Process • The importance of waiting for full disclosure • The pain of staggered disclosure • The danger of 'fishing for details' • Suggestions for disclosure to children	• *Journal* and *Workbook* questions related to waiting for full disclosure

RECOMMENDED READING/VIEWING

Exposed
👤 by James and Teri Craft
💲 $15.00
🖥 puredesire.org/exposed

Conquer Series DVD #2
👤 by KingdomWorks Studios
💲 $129.95
🖥 puredesire.org/conquer

ⓘ CONSIDER THIS

LESSON ONE

As an intro to Chapter 2, view DVD 2 of the Conquer Series about the brain. You may get push back from some women. They may think that we are making excuses for the addict's behavior. For that reason, it is important to help the wife understand: Once the addict understands how his brain has been changed, he will work diligently to renew his mind.

Jesus extends grace to the addict. It is grace that enables the addict to "go, and sin no more." Jesus speaks the truth without condemnation. In John 4 when Jesus is speaking to the woman at the well, she admits that she is living in sin—living with a man that is not her husband. Jesus offers living water; He offers grace, which allows and compels her to sin no more.

At this point in the process, we are not asking the wife to forgive. Forgiveness comes a few months down the road. However, we are cautioning her that shaming (shaming words—"How disgusting") will drive addiction. The wife needs to learn to share how hurtful his behavior is to her without shaming him. Shame will drive him further into his addiction. He already feels worthless. Therefore, words of shame or disgust will align with what the enemy is saying, rather than what God is calling him to.

In Lesson One of the *Betrayal & Beyond Journal*, we suggest asking women to "explain in your own words how a new understanding of grace might help prevent the acting in and acting out cycle."

HINT: WHAT DRIVES ADDICTION?
Answer: As women understand the noose of addiction, they will better understand the shame and worthlessness that the addict feels. That shame and worthlessness drive his sexual behavior. When he relapses and acts out, he will "put the lid on" and try hard not to do it again. Rather, he can receive God's grace; that grace gives him the ability to go and sin no more.

LESSON TWO

Helping the women understand abuse statistics is important. It is not an excuse for the addict's behavior. However, it helps them begin to understand that the addict is medicating the wounds of his past.

Some women may be so angry at their spouse that it may be difficult for them to even write out a prayer in their *Betrayal & Beyond Journal*. If that is the case, challenge them to journal the reason why it is so hard to write out a prayer at this point in their healing journey.

LESSON THREE

The primary goal of this lesson is to help women understand the limbic system. The limbic system (driven by feelings) will override the prefrontal cortex (higher reasoning) every time. It subconsciously hijacks the brain. In Seven Pillars of Freedom groups, men are learning to take that information and become self-aware. By using the FASTER Scale (introduced to the women in Chapter 5 of the *Betrayal & Beyond Workbook*), men are learning how to stop the downward spiral toward relapse.

LESSON FOUR

For those leaders who have not attended Pure Desire University training, and have not learned much about disclosure, we have provided extra information in the appendix. On page 77 is a worksheet to help women as they consider what they need to know for full disclosure—the Wife's Inventory for Disclosure. Remind them the more details they have, the harder it will be to re-engage with the addict, especially sexually. Many women who have demanded too many details say that is all they can think about when they are making love. However, she does need to know basics. Copy the Wife's Inventory for Disclosure if a group member is preparing for full disclosure. The resource isn't in the *Betrayal & Beyond Workbook* or *Journal* because we recommend that a pastor, counselor, Seven Pillars of Freedom group leader, or Betrayal & Beyond group leader go through the full disclosure with them.

During disclosure, we recommend that both the husband and the wife have the support of their group leaders and/or a counselor; although a certified sexual addiction therapist is preferred. Refer to puredesire.org to access staff CSATs, as well as CSAT Affiliates.

We recommend that the husband work through Pillars Five and Six of the Seven Pillars of Freedom before full disclosure takes place for three reasons:

1. The wife will begin to see a track record of sobriety and that real heart change is taking place.

2. Pillars Five and Six introduce with the Arousal Template and Trauma Timeline. These will help him discover traumas and sexual behaviors he has buried subconsciously for years.

3. There is less of a chance for staggered disclosure, because much of his conscious and unconscious behaviors will surface when he starts connecting the dots of trauma and arousal.

In the case that he has put her at risk for sexually transmitted diseases, disclosure should take place immediately, and they both need to be tested for STDs and HPV.

When telling the children, consider partnering with a counselor or pastor who understands sexual addiction. Disclosure to the children should take place after the couple has created a safe, healthy environment, and the addict has at least 6-12 months of sobriety. Disclosure to the children should be age appropriate. The children can be told, "Mom and Dad are in counseling to heal their marriage." They can also share, "Daddy has hurt Mommy. He lied to Mommy, and we want our marriage to change."

With older children, the couple may need to reveal more before full disclosure. In one case, a teen was upset that Covenant Eyes was put on his computer. He thought the parents didn't trust him. His dad had to confess that it was put on all computers because he was struggling. It wasn't about the son. This incident led to a positive conversation about dad's struggles and opened the door for the dad and his son to talk further on this topic.

CHAPTER THREE: COMMITMENT TO PERSONAL HEALING

In Chapter 3, women come to understand that they have played a part in the creation of the unhealthy dance in their marriage. They begin to see that their family history affects how they react to personal triggers. Group members learn to use the Karpman Triangle and the Double Bind to discover positive ways to express their needs.

LESSON	PRIMARY FOCUS	CONCEPTS & EXERCISES
❶ **What is Broken in Our Marriage?**	• Realizing she has a part in the unhealthy dance they created • Discovering places of brokenness and blind spots in her own life	• Cargo Ship drawing • Identifying areas of brokenness • Identifying areas she has tried to control & areas of vulnerability
❷ **What is Broken from My Past?**	• Investigating how your family history continues to influence and impact your present, both positively and negatively	• FACES Evaluation • Investigating Mother's and Father's role • Identifying patterns to keep and to change
❸ **What is Broken in Me?**	• Learning the difference between being a loving, kind and compassionate person and being codependent • Learning to use the tools of the Karpman Triangle and Double Bind to counteract codependency	• Codependent checklist • The Karpman Triangle • The Double Bind
❹ **What is Broken in My Spirit?**	• Identifying the lies the enemy has slipped into our minds because of the trauma we have endured, and learning to counter those lies with the Truth of God's Word	• Identifying lies of the enemy • Visual representations of personal trauma

RECOMMENDED READING/VIEWING

Disappointment with God
👤 by Philip Yancey

Families Where Grace Is in Place
👤 by Jeff VanVonderen

⚠ CONSIDER THIS

LESSON ONE

The main purpose of Chapter 3 is to help women understand that they have brought unhealthiness into the marriage too and she and her husband are doing a crazy dance, much of which they learned from their family of origin.

The focus of Chapter 1 and 2 has been on the addict and his issues. Now we are challenging the wife to look at herself and become more aware of her issues. **Remember: she is never to blame for his addiction, but she is involved in the crazy dance they have both learned to survive.**

At this point, the healing challenge will begin to focus on the wife. Her pain will be coming to the surface. Encourage the women to commit to calling each other two to three times a week. In Chapter 5, group members will be required to call each other weekly.

Chances are that this betrayal is not the first time. That understanding will prepare her to write her trauma timeline in Chapter 4. Until she understands that others have possibly betrayed and abandoned her, her husband could be the lightening rod for all her betrayals. We want her to separate him from past betrayals so that, when she starts working through the anger and forgiveness, she won't pile all the responsibility of her hurt on her husband.

....

LESSON TWO

This lesson will help her to honestly evaluate her family of origin. Addicts and their spouses often come from rigid, disengaged homes. Women have nothing to compare their family with so as they take the FACES Evaluation, they can see where their family of origin lines up. The purpose of this evaluation is not to blame mom and dad, but to see the patterns that have been passed on to subsequent generations. Until they see the pattern they can't change how they "do family."

If group members score in the very rigid and disengaged area of the chart, encourage them to ask their husband to take the FACES Evaluation. Additionally, the two of them could look at areas they need to change in their family situation.

Provide opportunity for them to share what they learned about their family of origin and themselves. It is important that group members understand that this is often the window they look through. Their views were given to them by their family of origin.

....

LESSON THREE

The Karpman Triangle will help women see how common it is to move from rescuer to victim in their relationship to the addict. This is a good lesson to come back and review when your group comes to the codependency lessons in Chapter 5. We often put three chairs in a triangle and put a sign on each one: rescuer, victim, and persecutor. We review a recent argument and have them sit on the victim or rescuer chair. Or, if they were the persecutor, we have them stand on that chair as they share what happened in the argument. They are amazed at how quickly they change chairs. You might want to have one woman share a recent argument and role play it with one of the other women playing the role of her spouse. We have more detailed information on this in the appendix, page

78. The appendix also explains how they can get off the triangle. While on the triangle they are going limbic (acting as children rather than adults). The person standing as the persecutor is more like a teenager, demanding what they want.

Moving forward, we will be providing more practice with the Double Bind tool. This is the only way group members understand the lose/lose situation they are in.

....

LESSON FOUR

This helps women deal with where they are with God. They grapple with why He allowed their situation to happen. *Disappointment with God* by Phillip Yancey will help them think through the fact that God never guaranteed that life would be fair. Although God doesn't cause the pain, He can turn it around for His glory and our good.

Another important concept in this lesson is: the Bible begins to make sense when you realize the finished work of grace is in your spirit, and the progressive work of grace is in your soul. Our soul—which includes our will, intellect, and emotions—needs to be converted. The hardware—or gateway—of your soul is your brain. This prepares group members to understand that there has to be a renewing of the mind: Romans 12:2.

The following are answers to the *Betrayal & Beyond Journal* questions:

SCRIPTURE	GOD'S CHARACTER	EFFECT ON MY OWN HEALING
Example: Exodus 15:22-26	*God is my healer*	*Regardless of my husband's choices, God is committed to my healing*
Jeremiah 33:14	God keeps His promise	
Psalms 10:14,17	God sees and hears me	
I John 1:9	God forgives and cleanses sin	
Ezekiel 48:35, Hebrews 13:5	God is with me—He will never leave nor abandon me	

SCRIPTURE	GOD'S POWER	HOPE IT BRINGS
Jeremiah 32:17	There is nothing too hard for God	
Ephesians 3:20	God can do beyond what I can think	
2 Peter 1:3	His power gives us all things pertaining to our life	

SCRIPTURE	GOD PROTECTS FROM	THEREFORE, I CAN RELEASE
Psalm 34:4	He heard me and delivered me from my fear	
Psalm 32:7	I can hide in You in times of trouble	
2 Thessalonians 3:3	He guards me from the evil one	

CHAPTER FOUR: TRAUMA'S UNDERCURRENT

During Chapter 4, group members will begin to focus less on the addict's addiction, and more on their own unhealthy behaviors. They will begin to identify how personal trauma has impacted them and discover destructive patterns and cycles that have been in place in their lives. They will begin to use a new tool, the Thankfulness Exercise, in their *Betrayal & Beyond Journals* to help them develop a thankful heart in order to combat negative thinking.

LESSON	PRIMARY FOCUS	CONCEPTS & EXERCISES
❶ What is Trauma?	• Discussing myths and facts about trauma • Exploring how past traumatic events of extreme impact ("whacks") and/or small wounds that occur repeatedly ("lacks") can trigger us to respond reactively or compulsively in the present	• Myths and truths about trauma • Personal "whacks and lacks" chart • Thankfulness Exercise
❷ Trauma's Influence in My Healing Journey	• Investigating how childhood issues from the past may affect a person in the present • Uncovering the participant's trauma story in order to become more self-aware • Discussion of PTSI areas of Trauma Reaction, Trauma Repetition, Trauma Bonds, and Trauma Shame	• PTSI evaluation and discussion of scores
❸ God's Grace Trumps Trauma	• Four concepts of emotional freedom • Discussion of PTSI areas of Trauma Pleasure, Trauma Blocking, Trauma Splitting, and Trauma Abstinence	• Discussion of PTSI scores
❹ Getting Unstuck from Trauma's Hold	• Brain development and trauma • Fight, flight or freeze as reactions to intense emotions • Identifying personal traumas	• Traumatic Events Chart • "Once upon a time there was a little girl..."

RECOMMENDED READING/VIEWING

The Betrayal Bond
👤 by Patrick Carnes

Conquer Series DVD #3
👤 by KingdomWorks Studios
💲 $129.95
🖥 puredesire.org/conquer

ⓘ CONSIDER THIS

Note: Chapters 4-6 may be more difficult and frustrating to women than the previous chapters. Remember that Chapters 1-2 dealt mostly with their husband's issues. For most women who struggle with codependency, solving his problems rather than looking at their own issues contribute to the destructive crazy dance they are involved in. Chapters 4-6 will bring up personal trauma, family or origin issues, and codependency. Many women become frustrated because this is the first time they have the mirror focused on them. Encourage them to realize how the *Betrayal & Beyond Journal* and the tools for identifying feelings in the *Workbook* appendix, pages 291-293 will be so important. Help them understand that many emotions may surface, and they will get more help dealing with emotions of loss, anger, and hurt when they get to Chapter 7.

LESSON ONE

The Conquer Series, DVD 3, focuses on how trauma affects addiction. The video does a great job of summarizing what group members have learned about addiction from Chapter 2, and summarizes much of what they will be learning in Chapter 4.

The purpose of this chapter is to help women understand that trauma can be highly intense or have low impact with frequency. Most of us think of huge trauma as events such as rape, loss of a parent, divorce, or near death experience. But most of us, unknowingly, experience little traumas over and over and don't recognize them. Those layers of even small traumas start adding up. So, when sexual behavior from the spouse is revealed it often sends women over the edge emotionally. Regardless of frequency and intensity, unresolved trauma compounds when it isn't processed in a healthy way. Some may have a difficult time identifying trauma. They often have lived with it for so long that they don't even recognize it. When you get to the Abuse Inventory in Chapter 6, encourage group members to come back to this lesson and see if they have left anything out.

Starting in Chapter 4 in the *Betrayal & Beyond Journal*, we are also asking women to write down 5 things they are thankful for each week. This would be a great way to open your meetings on a positive note. This exercise may be difficult for some women because they are so focused on their negative circumstances. The goal is to get them to lift their eyes above their circumstances and see what positive things God is doing. The truth is, God will always out do the enemy's bad with His good! We may have to look a little harder to see it.

LESSON TWO

The questions in this lesson are designed to help group members get in touch with childhood wounds. The concept of whacks and lacks will help them as they begin to create their Trauma Timeline. The timeline will help women see that over or under reactions in the present, could stem from their past. If they begin to connect these dots, the husband will not become the lightening rod for all their hurt, anger, and betrayal.

Note: After group members have completed the PTSI, demonstrate how to transfer their scores.

Remind them, if they scored 0-2 (low), this is not an area to focus on. If they scored 3-6 (moderate) they should explore strategies to resolve the past. If they scored 7-18 they may need clinical counseling besides the group experience.

The PTSI Analysis Overview is expanded in your appendix on page 71. It is a clinical overview that may help you give women more information about each of the trauma areas. We tried to simplify each of these areas with biblical truths within this chapter for group members.

In Lessons 2-3 of Chapter 4, group members will transfer the totals from each column from the Stress Index Answer Grid and record the total in each category. Each section is designed to give them specific information to process that area of trauma. They should only do the exercises in this section if they scored 3 or more. Note: there will be more resources in Lesson 4 of Chapter 4.

ADDITIONAL RESOURCES FOR GROUP LEADERS:

- **If there are high scores in TRT and/or TR**, that means trauma has happened over and over in their lives. Those with high Trauma Reaction (TRT) tend to be the women who are the most angry. If they are high in TRT and angry, but haven't scored high in other areas, they may be in denial. Encourage them to go back over some of the questions, especially in TR, TBD, and TS. Read down the column, asking them each of the questions out loud. It is recommended that women buddy up on the phone or in person to do this for TR, TBD, and TS to make sure that they answered them correctly, considering their entire lives. Often when you question them out loud, they put the pieces together. They realize why they react so strongly. Their trauma scores would be a great thing to discuss during weekly phone conversations.

- **Women struggling with a lot of codependency** usually score high in: TBD, they tend to be loyal to people who are untrustworthy; TS, they tend to feel a lot of shame in their relationships or blame themselves for things others have done to them, even as children; TB, they tend to find ways to avoid pain by using food, TV, or exercise to block the pain. Those who do extreme blocking might be high in TSG. Due to extreme abuse in childhood, they tend to check out of reality or daydream to avoid pain. Also, consistent with codependency is TA. These people have to work on self-care and have their small group hold them accountable to care for themselves. One of my group members would give all her weekly money allotment to others. Her self-esteem rested on how she could bless others. I asked her to only spend time/energy on herself for six months and have her group hold her accountable. Initially, she didn't think she could do it. This response showed how codependent she was and how dependent she was on others' validation to be okay.

LESSON THREE

In Lesson 3, we use Joseph's life to give hope in the midst of the traumatic issues they are facing. Even if things get worse (which they normally will), God will use the circumstance to strengthen them for His purpose for their lives. Whatever the enemy has meant for bad—God can turn to good!

Group members will still be transferring their scores to the last four trauma types. Trauma Blocking and Trauma Abstinence are often high among women married to addicts. If they are avoiding sex, their TA will be high. To some extent, that is normal with women who husbands have had extramarital relationships. Hopefully by Chapter 9, which focuses on healthy sexuality, they will be ready to talk about their sexual abstinence issue. If a group member sees no progress in this area, couples counseling would be beneficial. Those with a lot of previous trauma before marriage—especially abuse—might have a high Trauma Splitting (TSG) score. These women have learned how to disassociate when they are faced with pain (freeze). Women who have been betrayed rarely score high on TP

(Trauma Pleasure), unless they too are struggling with sexual or love addiction. If they have scored high in this area, they may want to join an Eight Pillars to Freedom group after Betrayal & Beyond.

....

LESSON FOUR

The purpose of this lesson is to help women begin to understand the Double Bind and how the hard thing to do is the right thing to do. Using the example of the Chinese handcuffs helps them to see that pulling away from the pain only locks them tighter into bondage to trauma. The way out is to press into the darkness, the pain, and what they have been running from. You may want to reference this lesson when we get to the FASTER Scale and the Double Bind.

Through Annie's story, we want them to see how they can easily put a parent's face on the face of God. In doing so, if we have the wrong God, we can never get free until we see God as full of grace, love, and willing to heal us at every point.

The questions about caretakers at an early age, both for them and their husband, helps identify what kind of attachments they had early in life. Group members with negative or very little attachments, tend to become easily angered in relationship (puff up), or tend to isolate (shrink back). Thus, they will overreact or underreact to situations in life. Past trauma is literally driving their limbic responses to "fight" or "flight."

Understanding past pain in the form of whacks or lacks impact their present if not dealt with. Therefore, we are asking them to begin going back and recording those times.

This exercise will help them write their trauma stories in their *Betrayal & Beyond Journal*. Explain that their story needs to be about 3-4 minutes with these guidelines:

- Your Trauma Chart from Lesson 4 can help you include significant elements for your story.

- Suggested length of your story: 700 words or less.

- Start your story with: "Once upon a time there was a little girl…"

- Read your story after it is completed. Journal at the end of the story about how you felt as you read about the little girl in the story.

- Be prepared to share it with ladies in your group the next time you meet.

Explain that they will be reading the story without stopping to make comments. Encourage them to practice reading it before they share with the group. Plan to spend a few minutes after each to ask them what they were feeling as they read their little girl story; what they were feeling for that little girl. Also, ask others in the group how they felt as they listened to her story; they will add more empathetic statements that the storyteller may never have heard from her parents. This will help her receive what she should have received from her caregivers.

CHAPTER FIVE: UNTANGLING UNHEALTHY RELATIONSHIPS

Throughout the five lessons of Chapter 5, group members will continue to dig deeper to identify and address codependency in their lives. They learn about their own personal coping mechanisms and patterns. Women will begin to understand how to use the FASTER Scale and the Double Bind exercises to help them become more self-aware and aid their healing process.

LESSON	PRIMARY FOCUS	CONCEPTS & EXERCISES
❶ Is It Trauma or Codependency?	• A need for safety and/or a need for control can motivate our behaviors in response to the addict's behavior • Trauma and Codependency can overlap	• Identifying behavioral motivation • Identifying trauma-related behaviors in biblical characters • Trauma Timeline
❷ The Mask of Codependency	• Defining codependency • Codependency, controlling, and rescuing behaviors as an attempt to manage the husband's addiction • Carrying each other's burdens, but allowing each to carry their own load • Natural consequences: The law of sowing and reaping	• Codependency Checklist • Identifying areas to change
❸ Losing Yourself Behind the Mask	• The roots of codependency • Concept of using masks to hide our insecurities and give a false sense of control	• Review FACES exercise • Exploring the masks we wear
❹ Lifting the Mask to Heal the Wounds	• Choosing to believe God's truths about me • Limbic lies are only changed through new and opposite experiences	• God's Truth Mirror • Who I Am In Christ
❺ God Esteem: Your True Identity	• "God Esteem" is who God says you are and is a powerful weapon against the enemy • Understanding the power of God's Personal Promises • Discussing the FASTER Scale and the Double Bind exercise	• FASTER Scale • Double Bind Exercise • Personal Promises

RECOMMENDED READING/VIEWING

Untangling Relationships
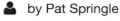 by Pat Springle

ⓘ CONSIDER THIS

LESSON ONE

How will you spend time going through the women's stories? If you have a large group, you may want to do half this week and the rest of the stories next week. Remind group members they will be reading their stories and not commenting as they read. This will help manage time and have a greater impact. However, the group should ask: how did that make you feel? Ask how they felt as they were sharing. Ask other group members what they felt as they were hearing the story. Often the storyteller has no idea how traumatic their story is until they see others responding with tears or gasps and comments. Those feelings are important to identify and express.

Many object to the label of codependency. We want to make sure we never label women. As the women process these five lessons in Untangling Unhealthy Relationships, we want them to grapple with what codependency is and define if they are reacting out of trauma, codependent behavior, or a combination of the two. If we allow women to self-define their issues, they will be able to see the coping mechanisms they use to protect themselves, as well as remain safe.

Abigail's story is used as a biblical example. Group members may struggle with how a woman in that culture is different than today. Abigail was running her house hold and manipulating (working around her husband to rescue everyone), which would be highly unusual for that culture.

In Lesson 2, the Codependency Test will help women identify a lot of the behaviors; their tendency is to use those behaviors to feel safe. It is also important to state that 15% of women who are married to addicts are not codependent.

Here are some possible answers that ladies might give as to why David and the woman at the well were experiencing certain trauma's listed in the trauma index. The purpose of this exercise is to help group members identify the types of trauma in their life and their spouse's life. Unlike Abigail who was married to an addict, these examples are more from the addict's experience. They can help women have more empathy for their spouse. Group members will have an opportunity to express their response to David and the woman at the well in more depth in their *Betrayal & Beyond Journal*.

IDENTIFYING TRAUMA EXERCISE—SUGGESTED ANSWERS:

David:

1. Trauma Repetition and/or Trauma Shame: by family members
2. Trauma Bond: Loyalty to Saul, his king and father-in-law, who is dangerous
3. Trauma Pleasure/Trauma Blocking: Used when David sought relief of pain through pleasure and risk. Also possibly Trauma Blocking, if he used the affair to block the pain

Woman at the Well:

1. Trauma Shame: She feels worthless due to her lifestyle.
2. Trauma Repetition/Trauma Blocking: Observed in her repeated behavior and sexual relationships to block the pain
3. Trauma Repetition/Trauma Pleasure/Trauma Blocking: Exhibited as she continues to risk her well being and reputation to medicate through repeated relationships in attempts to block the pain
4. Trauma Blocking/Trauma Shame: Because of the shame she feels—she quickly turns the conversation to religion—she uses her religious knowledge to block and numb the pain brought up with discussion of her inappropriate relationships.

Have your timeline done to show them and give them examples of what theirs could look like. Divide your life into four sections and fill in the trauma and the lies associated with that trauma (if you are 40 years old, the first box would include your history from 0-10; the second box ages 11-20, etc.).

Remind group members that they can't change their trauma history. However, they can change the lies that are attached to that history. We will come back to this chapter to help them identify the lies Hell attached to the traumas, and help them identify their prophetic promises. These encounters they have with God when He tells them who they are, will be the new messages to replace the lies. In the next lesson, the beliefs behind the mask will help them to further identify lies attached to their trauma experiences.

LESSON TWO

It is important that women self diagnose their own issues. Some women have learned different survival techniques that have made them a perfect fit for the addict; behaviors such as rescuing, walking on eggshells, and controlling to keep him sober.

Using the biblical story of Rebekah will help ladies recognize that Rebekah was trusting her own problem-solving, rather than allowing God to fulfill His promise. Additionally, the scripture in Galatians (developed more in Chapter 6), will help them begin to think through boundaries.

The Simple Codependency Checklist is designed to help break denial in women who don't realize some of their behaviors are codependent. Having them share their discoveries from the test will help them become more self aware and familiar with codependent habits.

LESSON THREE

The purpose of this lesson is to help women go deeper into what codependency is and how it might be evident in their lives. We first look at Danae's story to help them begin to identify codependent behaviors.

Help them identify the link between past and present trauma and family of origin issues to present patterns in their life that are reactions to their wounds and fears.

Using the Mask Chart will help group members connect the fear or lies they believe and some of their codependent coping mechanisms. They may be referring back to these as they begin to uncover their distorted belief system. In the next lesson, we want to help them find prophetic promises (personal promises) to counteract the lies Hell has tied to their wounds.

The TrueFaced video is a great resource.[11] Either show the video during this lesson or challenge them to watch it on their own. In this Youtube video, John Lynch challenges us to stop trying to please God (by wearing masks) and take a new path of trusting God (taking off the masks).

---

11. John Lynch. TrueFaced Two Roads Message, 2012. https://www.youtube.com/watch?v=Rfy03PEVUhQ.

LESSON FOUR

This week is crucial in helping women deal with the wounds of the past and the present. We can't change our history, but we can change the lies we believe that drive our behavior. In the two steps provided, we ask women to identify the lies they have believed about themselves. Some of those lies have come out as they have been doing different lessons; especially in Lesson 3, as they have identified the masks they tend to wear. Provide group members with examples from your life.

Step two is crucial. For some women this may be a new experience. We are trying to communicate that the only way a lie is truly changed is through a new limbic spiritual experience with God. Encourage group members to make a commitment this week to spend time before the Lord asking Him for new pictures. He may have revealed things to them in their past, but they weren't able to recognize that the encounter was provided to help them challenge the lie they believed.

It is important to couple the experience with the word of God. The activities in the *Betrayal & Beyond Journal* are very important this week. Group members will need to identify the lie, then journal what they hear God say and record it in their *Workbook*. Finally, they will use their *Journal* to identify the *logos* word from Scripture to record in their *Workbooks*. They should try to repeat this exercise with at least three lies. There is a list of Scriptures in their *Journal* for this week that might fit the experience they had with God and would reinforce who God says they are.

Starting next week we are going to ask them to rehearse these truths daily so that they know them by heart. This exercise will help them renew their mind and pray in light of their promises rather than their problems.

....

LESSON FIVE

This week, our goal is to give the women an opportunity to better understand their personal/prophetic promises and add any new promises. It is also designed to help them see how powerful these promises can become in their warfare against the enemy.

If you stop and think through your life, you will be able to identify several times where God powerfully met you through His Holy Spirit. It may have been during a time of tragedy, pain, or great rejoicing. In these moments, God was revealing not only His character, but also His view of you. You can take these encounters, pair them with Scripture, and create a God-given, personal vision of who you are in Christ.

They are learning "practices" that must be done daily for the renewing of the mind. Daily, they are to give thanks for specific things that God is doing. Remind them that because of past trauma, our brains will default to looking for that which is harmful, unsafe, or negative. With their promises identified, they can begin to pray in light of them rather than their problems.

In Lesson 5, we add the FASTER Scale. This is a weekly exercise—possibly more than just once a week—if they are going through crisis. As group members are beginning to understand their FASTER Scale, we want them to commit to calling the women in their group at least three times a week. This practice will help them avoid isolation and challenge them to share where they are on the FASTER Scale. With the support of the women in their group, women can help each other understand the Double Bind they are facing and why they are going down the FASTER Scale.

Provide personal examples from your own FASTER Scale. Share three characteristics of what you would write out in each category. The hardest issue might be relapse. They probably don't see how addicted they are to controlling situations, rescuing, or dark thinking. Ask them to describe when they feel hopeless and what they do in those situations. That is their relapse.

There are listed meditation Scriptures for each of the FASTER Scale categories. Encourage the women to identify the area they are struggling with most (i.e. Anxiety or Ticked Off). Prompt them to journal after the Scripture in that category. Ongoing, remind them to return to these Scriptures for comfort and help when they fill out the FASTER Scale.

This is the first week we introduce the Courageous Commitment to Change. It appears in their *Betrayal & Beyond Journal*. It requires an accountability person that will ask them how they are doing on their commitments. We will add a worksheet next time, as well as a Group Check-in sheet. Explain these tools with them in preparation for your Lesson 1 meeting in Chapter 6. Remind them to do at least one FASTER Scale and Double Bind each week.

COMMITMENT TO COURAGEOUSLY CHANGE THIS WEEK:

1. I will give thanks each day.
2. I will rehearse my promises.
3. I will call three women this week.
4. I will share my FASTER Scale & Double Bind this week.

Who will hold you accountable? _____

CHAPTER SIX: HEALTHY BOUNDARIES

In Chapter 6, group members are learning to develop healthy boundaries. They will explore the difference between healthy/safe and unhealthy/unsafe relationships. They will understand that they have the personal power of choosing vulnerability and closeness with others.

LESSON	PRIMARY FOCUS	CONCEPTS & EXERCISES
❶ Steps to the New Dance: Boundaries	• What are boundaries? What does the Bible say about boundaries? • Healthy boundaries increase our ability to care about others and our ability to care for ourselves	• Identifying boundaries
❷ Steps to the New Dance: Balance	• Overfunctioning and underfunctioning • The Karpman Triangle • Recognizing abuse in our history	• Teeter-Totter Diagram • Double Bind Exercise • Abuse Inventory • Drawing Exercise: Life With and Without Healthy Boundaries
❸ Steps to the New Dance: My Safety Plan	• Establishing healthy boundaries by creating the Safety Plan	• Safety Plan
❹ Stepping Out with New Dance Moves	• Importance of following through with your Safety Plan and allowing natural consequences to take place • The teeter-totter analogy: ups and downs in the healing process within the marriage	• Safety Plan • Teeter-Totter Exercise

RECOMMENDED READING/VIEWING

Boundaries in Marriage
👤 by Henry Cloud and John Townsend

CONSIDER THIS

LESSON ONE

Our goal in this lesson and the next is to help women find their voice. Many women don't realize how they have allowed others, including the addict, to run over their boundaries. Many women may have small emotional abuses that take place daily and they don't realize it. The end of the next lesson will help group members identify abuses that have been taking place.

We are also trying to balance out the "doormat Christianity." That perspective is often communicated as a virtue. In that case, many women do not have a two-way relationship, but are usually the ones always giving. When that dynamic exists with the addict and she discovers betrayal, it can often create more anger. She thought she was doing the "Christian" thing, but has come to find out he was using it to help feed his addiction. Help women get in touch with their feelings about boundary busters.

Use the teeter-totter to demonstrate the people in her life that she has allowed to dominate her with overfunctioning.

LESSON TWO

In their *Betrayal & Beyond Journal* this week, we are having group members do two Double Binds on overfunctioning and underfunctioning. From here on out, to help them get off their FASTER Scale, this Double Bind will be available every lesson.

Remind the women that each week we are asking them to write down at least four promises and Scripture. We want them to know these so they can recite them and use them when they are feeling fearful or under attack. Also, rehearsing them each morning helps women start the day believing the truth about who God says they are.

In the *Workbook*, the teeter-totter helps women understand the Karpman Triangle. Group members are asked to identify people who overfunction (those who tend to control others overtly like persecutors or covertly like rescuers). Those that are underfunctioning tend to be victims and avoid conflict at all cost. They often walk on eggshells around the addict. Although all of us may operate at either end of the teeter-totter, help the women identify which one best describes them in most of their relationships.

If women check the violations—especially physical and possibly sexual abuse—they might need to get counseling or help from a Domestic Violence group in your state. Help them fill out step 4 in the next lesson if you think their life might be at risk.

LESSON THREE

Make sure you are ready to share your own Safety Plan with the women in your group. Go step by step helping them to fill out and discuss each step.

Note: Only the first three steps need to be filled out—unless a woman is separated already and/or is in an abusive situation, which you would have discovered by their scores from the previous lesson on abuse. Women in this category may need to look at steps 4-7. This will help them prepare for situations beyond the normal. It may be that the husband refuses to get help and is threatening to choose his addiction or the other woman over the wife. Hopefully, if any of these scenarios are taking place, she is seeking professional counseling in addition to attending the group. Domestic violence resources are available to support and help her if she or her children are at risk.

Walk through the *Betrayal & Beyond Journal* for that week. The Safety Plan is their homework and focus this week. Help them to understand that not all the options apply to them. This plan can change as the spouse becomes more trustworthy. Women can make copies of the Safety Plan in the *Betrayal & Beyond Workbook* on page 177 or download a copy from puredesire.org/bb-resources to update their Safety Plan as they see their spouse making significant changes. Because this is a three to five year process, we encourage women to evaluate and, if necessary, make changes every six to nine months, even after their Betrayal & Beyond group has ended. We encourage them to fill it out after they complete the Pure Desire groups. We will talk more about the Safety Plan later in the *Betrayal & Beyond Workbook*.

....

LESSON FOUR

In this lesson, group members will each be sharing their Safety Plans. In places they aren't sure how to complete, let the group help them; especially, figuring out reasonable consequences. The wife, in her anger, may not even see that she is being punitive. Allow the group to call her on it. Or, she may not have reached her bottom line. If there is another affair or prostitute, what is she willing to do? Whatever she puts in her Safety Plan, she must be willing to follow through. Challenge women who come up with extreme consequences to consider that fact as she creates her Safety Plan.

We want to underline the importance of natural consequences and help the women see how important it is for them to be willing to follow through with these consequences. The tendency is two extremes: overreacting and threatening to leave, or divorce, or underreacting and allowing abusive behavior to continue. In the latter case, once she finds her voice, she may swing to the other end of the spectrum and become vocally abusive. This will only drive the addict further away. She doesn't have to go to either extreme. When a violation takes place, she pulls out the Safety Plan and follows it. She will need women in the group to help her follow through. Also, it is important for her to realize every six months she needs to review and update her Safety Plan. **Caution:** it shouldn't be updated in the middle of a consequence. Otherwise, to the addict it will look like she is easy to manipulate.

Talk about the teeter-totter and the new dance the women are learning. Have each member of the group select which teeter-totter she can identify with the most. How has it made her feel as they worked through the segment? Most women are relieved that the ups and downs they are going through are normal. The purpose of this section is to help group members realize that learning a new way of relating is awkward and hurtful at times. But, eventually things will change; especially if both her and her spouse are committed to the process of healing.

We will go back to the teeter-totter example as we work our way through Chapters 7-9.

CHAPTER SEVEN: FACING MY GRIEF AND ANGER

By this point, women are ready to begin learning how to process their grief and anger in more healthy ways. They will be able to identify the difference between real and perceived losses, understand the issues surrounding repressed anger, and be able to express the reality of how betrayal has affected their life.

LESSON	PRIMARY FOCUS	CONCEPTS & EXERCISES
❶ The Stages of Grief	• Identifying losses due to the betrayal and facing the reality of what has been lost • Stages of Grief and the feelings commonly experienced within each stage	• Letter to "The Man I Thought I Married"
❷ Unhealthy Anger	• How to evaluate the results of the Anger Test • Repressed anger • The Unhealthy Anger Cycle: I React	• The Anger Test
❸ Healthy Anger	• Using The Healthy Anger Cycle: I Respond • The HALT acronym • Strategies for healthy demonstration of anger	• Picture • Letter to "The Man I Realize I Married"
❹ Grieving Your Losses	• Grief is a process, not a one-time event • Grief comes in layers • Dealing with profound sadness in healthy ways • Cooperating with God as He transforms our sorrow into joy	• Physical activity to grieve and release the loss

RECOMMENDED READING/VIEWING

A Grace Disguised: How the Soul Grows through Loss
👤 by Jerry L. Sittser

⊙ CONSIDER THIS

LESSON ONE

As they share their losses from this week's lesson, there will probably be a lot of tears. As they cry, be prepared to allow time to pray over them, especially as they read their letter: The man I thought I married. Allow three minutes for each woman to read their letter. Emphasis that they need to read and not stop to provide explanation. Remember, when the women read the illusion of "The Man I Thought I Married" they are saying goodbye to that illusion. Ask the following questions:

- Before you read to the group for three minutes, tell us what you were feeling as you were writing your letter.

- What did you feel as you just read—the illusion you were saying goodbye to?

- Then ask others how they felt as she read her letter.

Help them think through the Stockdale Paradox and state specifically the tensions each of them are facing. What is the specific pain? What is the hope they are holding onto? Refer to what they wrote in their *Betrayal & Beyond Journal*.

Throughout Chapters 7-9, we will be asking women to identify their feelings. Continually point them to Chart of Primary, Secondary, and Tertiary Emotions in the appendix of the *Workbook,* page 292.

LESSON TWO

Be sure and help the women look at their Anger Test results in light of Boundary and Self-Esteem issues listed after the test. If the numbers in each of the categories are high, they may be indicators of attitudes and behaviors that lead to codependent behavior.

You may need to use this lesson to have women finish reading their letter "To The Man I Thought I Married." Follow the instructions in Lesson 1.

As they walk through the "Unhealthy Anger Cycle: I React" remind them to use the feelings charts in the appendix of their *Workbook,* pages 291-293. Point out that this Unhealthy Anger Cycle is missing a number of steps that will be covered in the next lesson, "When I skip steps, I will end up Reacting rather than Responding."

LESSON THREE

They will begin writing their stories: "The Man I Realized I Married" this week. The purpose for this exercise is two-fold: first, we want to help group members get rid of the illusions that they presented in their first letter of "The Man I Thought I Married." Second, we want to start identifying their losses and the anger they have experienced. They may need more pages than their *Betrayal & Beyond Journal* allows to write out all their anger. We encourage them to create a rough draft in another notebook, then synthesize it down to three pages that take three minutes to read. Reminder: not all their husband's traits and behaviors were lies. But right now, that may be hard to separate, especially if he has not engaged in the healing process. In a few weeks, we will be looking at "The Man I See You Becoming." If the husband is in the healing process, group members should be able to recognize some visible changes.

Challenge the women to think through and commit to healthy ways they can deal with their anger. Encourage other group members to hold them accountable this week. This could be part of their Courageous Commitment to Change for next week.

....

LESSON FOUR

Have the women read their stories: "The Man I Realize I Married." Ask them how they felt as they wrote it. After reading it in the group, ask them how they felt while they were reading it. Ask the group how they felt hearing her read it aloud.

After they share their painful letters, have group members write out their losses from all the lessons they have done. Come prepared with sticky notes—give at least ten to each woman. If possible play some soft music in the background and let them write down from Lesson 1 what they are willing and ready to lay at the cross (either have a miniature cross or draw one on a flipchart or whiteboard). After they have written out their losses—one sticky note for each loss—instruct them (when they are ready) to stick it on or at the foot of the cross. Let them know that this is an act of faith. Some may not be able to let go of all the sticky notes and that is okay. If they are not ready to let go of some have them put them in their *Betrayal & Beyond Journal*. Encourage them to write about that specific note, asking God to help them to let go and trust Him. They may not have to say goodbye to a marriage (like Shelby did in her story at the beginning of this lesson), but help them list those things they are letting go of and trusting God for.

Help the women identify the correlation between Gerald Sittser's running from the darkness and the Chinese handcuffs. Gerald was running to get away from the darkness—the pain—when we pull hard on the handcuffs we stay locked into the pain. As we push our fingers together into the pain (darkness), we find release.

From these options in their *Workbooks*, have them find and commit to one of the ways of dealing with their loss and anger. Have them select someone to keep them accountable; this could be included in their Courageous Commitment to Change this week.

❯ Find a way to do something physical that represents giving your losses to the Lord. Which ones are you ready to offer to God? The following are a few activity ideas:

Gather small rocks, each one representing one of your losses. Find a quiet setting, alone or with your small group. Physically take your rocks, name each one, and place them under a cross or in a bowl that you want to offer as a sacrifice to Christ. It is important to **be specific as you name each loss**. Then, pray. Ask Jesus to transform them into hope and joy in the way that only He can (Psalm 18).

If you have a safe place, like a barbeque or fire pit, write each of your losses on separate slips of paper. Be specific and intentional about throwing each one into the fire and watch as it is consumed and becomes ashes. (Please be very careful; only do this in a safe place outdoors). After you have put all of your notes into the fire, pray and ask Jesus to turn your ashes into beauty. Remember, Jesus came "*to give you the oil of gladness instead of mourning and a garment of praise instead of a spirit of despair*" (Isaiah 6:1-3).

Read the letter you have written over the last several weeks to the group. Then shred it or burn it. Use the same process and cautions in previous suggestion (Isaiah 6:1-3).

Teri: I sometimes wrap myself in a shawl and imagine curling up in the loving arms of Father God and allow Him to hold me as I talk to Him about my pain, my hurt, fears, and loss (Zephaniah 3:17).

Here is another option that is a little different than the sticky notes that helps women realize the weight we carry when we don't yield our burdens to the Lord. In Chapter 8, we begin to grapple with forgiveness. This might be a great exercise for your group:

WHAT'S IN YOUR BACKPACK?

Teri: I have learned by experience, that doing something physically to represent what is being done spiritually is a powerful way for my mind and heart to embrace reality. In your group, ask one of the ladies to come up front and put on a cute little "Winnie-the-Pooh" backpack. The backpack is empty and she tells us that it is no problem to carry.

One-by-one the women place fist-sized rocks into the backpack as they say words that represent things they may believe or feel, or a guilt or shame put upon them by others. The rocks represent sadness, loss, lies, and burdens that betrayal brings. Picture a rock being dropped into the backpack as each of these statements is spoken:

- **Rock 1** - "I will hide the secret from my friends and family. I feel so ashamed; I must keep this a secret."

- **Rock 2** - "I will lose weight and never make him angry. That will keep him from doing it again. I can keep our family together."

- **Rock 3** - "I will explain to the kids what daddy really meant when he was yelling at them, what he meant to say when he was being so critical."

- **Rock 4** - "I will show him how to recover from this addiction; I will read every book on men's sexual addiction that I can find. I will even take the tests for him and then show him what he needs to do to overcome this."

- **Rock 5** - "I have to make up for the losses my kids have gone through. I know! I'll buy that expensive equipment they've been wanting!"

- **Rock 6** - "If I were just a more submissive wife like it talks about in the Bible, he would never feel the need to do such a thing!"

- **Rock 7** - "I'd better watch for him! Oh, there is a billboard with a scantily clad lady! I'll distract him… Man! That girl's clothes are so tight! Oh, no, we're driving right by a strip joint! I forgot to go on the other road…"

By now, the cute little backpack is getting very heavy. When we ask the group member wearing it about the difference between carrying the backpack empty or with added weight, she typically tells us, "It is getting hard to carry. It is hurting my shoulders and back. I don't think I could walk very long carrying this load."

With a cross at the far side of the room, we ask her if she would like to give her burden to Jesus. She walks across the room, removes the bulging backpack, and places it at the foot of the cross. At this point, she and many women are in tears at the reality of all of the things that are stuffed into our own "backpacks," weighing us down. We then turn down the lights, play worship music, light candles, and each woman writes on slips of paper the things in her backpack that she is ready and willing to take to the cross.

I encourage you to do this with your small group. Using fist-sized large rocks (approximately the size of small oranges), tape onto each rock a note with things that are in your "backpack." Write things that you have believed you had to do or that others said you must do, that should not have been yours to carry. Write your losses and your "raw materials" on rocks, too. Then, put that backpack on. (*Do not do this if you cannot lift the backpack, or have now or have ever had any kind of back problem*). Have other ladies read the items you wrote out loud and then drop each rock into the backpack. Allow yourself to experience, physically, how difficult it is to carry the burdens that God never designed for you to carry.

If you do the Rock Exercise, encourage the women to journal what they have experienced and let that be part of your discussion next week.

CHAPTER EIGHT: HEALING AND FORGIVENESS

Group members are now ready to explore the concept of forgiveness. They will understand the concept of true forgiveness, recognizing the difference between forgiveness and reconciliation. They will come to recognize the effect of their past traumas on their ability to forgive, and be able to make choices about how and when to forgive those who have wronged them.

LESSON	PRIMARY FOCUS	CONCEPTS & EXERCISES
❶ What is Forgiveness?	• Myths and truths about forgiveness • The difference between forgiveness and reconciliation	• Identifying My Past Hurts • Letters to those who have hurt me
❷ Why Should I Forgive?	• The purpose and process of forgiveness • Working through forgiveness is a spiritual battle • Benefits of forgiveness	• Identifying benefits of forgiving
❸ Whom Do I Forgive?	• Identifying those we need to forgive, including others, God and ourselves • Determining whether you are ready to forgive or not • Bitterroot judgments and vows • Grace is the opposite of judgments	• Identifying people I need to forgive • Identifying vows or judgments I have made
❹ How Do I Forgive?	• Forgiveness is choice, not an emotion • Forgiveness first occurs between you and God • Forgiving someone should be very specific • Obstacles to forgiveness: vows, judgments, and soul-ties	• Proxy Exercise • Renouncing soul-ties

RECOMMENDED READING/VIEWING

An Affair of the Mind
👤 by Laurie Hall

The Power of a Praying Wife
👤 by Stormie Omartian

⊙ CONSIDER THIS

LESSON ONE

If you did the "Sticky Notes on the Cross" or the "Rock Exercise" suggested in Chapter 7, encourage the women to share what they journaled—what they experienced—and let that be part of your discussion as you begin this lesson.

The next four lessons are probably the hardest lessons for women to process. Some have prematurely forgiven. Though they have gone through the anger, loss, and now the forgiveness chapters, they may see new anger emerging. Let them know that mentally (left brain) they may have forgiven because it was the "Christian thing" to do or they were caught up in the myths we describe in this chapter.

We are now working on the emotional forgiveness (right brain). Some might not be ready to forgive. As group members finish all four lessons in Chapter 8, some will still not be ready to forgive. They may have to repeat this lesson. Many women are numb for the first three months of the group. We encourage women to find something to forgive; it might be something small. Through these lessons they will have an opportunity to record the specific things they are willing to forgive. This is a process. Hopefully, group members will come back to the unprocessed hurts at a later date and fully forgive those too.

In this lesson, the women will be focused on people who have hurt or wounded them in their past. The following lessons will focus specifically on their present betrayal. This is important. If women don't see that they have been wounded, betrayed, and even abandoned in their past, they will tend to focus all their anger on their spouse. We want them also to notice patterns. If they scored high on TBD (Betrayal Bonds) in Chapter 4, chances are, there have been a number of people they have been loyal to that betrayed them.

LESSON TWO

The main purpose of this lesson is to help women see the benefits of forgiveness through God's Word.

The other purpose is to help them see that their spouse is not the only one who has hurt them through the years. There could be repeated patterns of hurt throughout the wife's entire life.

During discussion time, probe into the benefits of forgiveness according to Scripture.

Ask the women to share personal experiences where they have seen the benefits of forgiveness in their own lives. You might even have some share a Double Bind about forgiving someone who has deeply hurt them.

See if any group members are ready to tackle the list of hurts from the previous lesson and begin to write letters.

LESSON THREE

The main purpose in this lesson is to help women be specific about who they need to forgive: people from their past and present, themselves, and God. By giving them charts to use, they can check off if they are ready to forgive. For some women, this may seem impossible at this point. If that is the case, encourage them to look for one or two people they can forgive. Remind them that forgiveness is a process much like peeling an onion.

The second purpose is to help women understand the vows and/or judgments they have made to protect themselves and recognize that these decisions have kept them stuck in unhealthy patterns. We have given general examples of vows and/or judgments so that group members can recognize what they have believed. Hopefully, they can come up with others that have literally become curses to them.

Encourage them, like Erica, (the last testimony in the *Workbook*) to go before God and ask Him where He was in their darkest pain. Pray that God would give each of the women new revelation of His care and protection over them.

Have women read their "letting go" prayer out loud. Encourage them to come back to this from time to time and see if they can check off any other statements of letting go as they progress through their healing. Point out that most of the letting go statements indicate codependent rescuing. If they struggle with checking them off, they may need to go back and review Chapters 5 and 6 which deal with codependency and healthy boundaries.

....

LESSON FOUR

The Proxy Exercise is powerful. Provide time so that group members can pair up, sit knee to knee with someone else, and go through—step by step—what is laid out in their *Betrayal & Beyond Journal*.

Breaking the power of soul-ties is important for the husband if there has been infidelity, as well as the wife if she has engaged in sex with anyone other than her husband. Encourage women to pray these prayers for themselves if that is the case. Also, because these prayers are in the husband's *Seven Pillars of Freedom Workbook*, it is important for them to discuss this together in order to achieve healing for their marriage.

You might want to use the example with the pink piece of paper glued to the blue piece of paper to illustrate what I shared concerning soul-ties. I encourage you to glue it and pull it apart before the group time. During group just hold them together and take them apart so they can see what happened to the pink and blue when they were previously glued together. It might take a few tries to get the glue to dry just right—so that when you pull them apart some of the pink stays stuck to the blue and vice versa. It's okay if it even tears a little since that is what sex outside the marriage does— there is a tearing effect on all involved.

Encourage the women to go through the Letting Go poem in their *Betrayal & Beyond Journal* and mark the areas they are letting go of. **You might want to plan a "Letting Go Party" for next week.** Provide environmental friendly helium balloons for each woman to write on what they are letting go. Before the release, have each woman express what they are letting go and trusting God with. Women often comment that a physical expression of what they are doing spiritually, really helps them move forward into what God has for them.

CHAPTER NINE: RESTORING HEALTH AND CLOSENESS

As the women approach the end of the *Workbook*, they are learning the steps toward restoring health and closeness in their relationships. They are able to identify and pursue the next, healthy steps for healing and growth. They realize the importance of developing and maintaining a healthy support system as they move forward.

LESSON	PRIMARY FOCUS	CONCEPTS & EXERCISES
❶ The Addict's Perspective	• Men's Panel: Discussion of their perspectives	• Letter To "The Man I See You Becoming"
❷ The Wife's Perspective: Should I Stay or Should I Leave?	• Review the Safety Plan for any fine-tuning that may need done • Divorce is the last resort and should have biblical grounds • Characteristics of safe and unsafe people • Importance of self-care	• Final Collage • Reviewing Safety Plan • Identifying Safe and Unsafe actions of spouse and self • Brené Brown: BRAVING
❸ A Healthy Marriage Perspective on Intimacy and Sex	• Nonsexual Pursuit: What does it look like? • How to determine if she is ready to move toward sexual intimacy • Understanding healthy and unhealthy sexuality • The difference between male and female approaches to intimacy	• Suggestions for Pursuing • Developing Intimacy Exercise • Thankfulness Exercise • Courageous Commitment to Change • FASTER Scale
❹ A Perspective for the Future	• Creating a target for a healthy new lifestyle: Three Circles Exercise • Identifying your weapons against the enemy: Defeating the Assaults From Hell • Discovering Your Dreams: Identifying the gifts God has given you and thinking about your legacy	• Three Circles Exercise • Drawing Exercise: Your Legacy • Plan to continue walking in "Corporate Anointing" • Couple's Safety Plan • Thankfulness Exercise

RECOMMENDED READING/VIEWING

Safe People
 by Henry Cloud and John Townsend

Anatomy of Trust
by Brené Brown

CONSIDER THIS

LESSON ONE

This lesson is a summary of a 90 minute *Betrayal & Beyond DVD* that is available for you to order at puredesire.org. You may want to play portions of it so that your group members can actually see the couples to which we are referring. The DVD also contains two seven-minute testimonies of two different marriages. One marriage survived the sexual addiction; the other did not. These testimonies could be shared in Chapter 9, Lesson 2, or they could be shared when you start your next group.

This week group members will identify where their marriage is in light of the panel members who shared. One of the main purposes for this week is to support their Safety Plan. Every one of the men in the DVD didn't like it at first, but eventually realized that as the wife followed through, her Safety Plan was key to their healing.

This lesson may be difficult for those whose marriages have ended. Remind those women to take time to hear the responses of the panel members, especially if they plan to ever marry again. The women's choice to walk in health now and in the future can set the stage for what God has for them. Encourage them to respond to Teri's testimony at the end of their lesson in their *Betrayal & Beyond Journal*.

In this lesson, we are challenging the women to begin writing their final letter to their spouse: "To The Man I See You Becoming." Impress upon them the importance of looking for small steps, how important this is for them to focus on some of the positive (Philippians 4:8), and for their spouse to hear she is noticing their progress. If women whose marriages have ended share custody of their children, we encourage them to write a prayer asking God to help him become the man their children need as a father. Allow time next week for the women to read what they have written or give them an extra week and do it in week three of this chapter.

This is also a great time to have group members begin to think about what they are going to do when this group ends. Just as the healing journey is a 3-5 year process for the addict, she is also having to walk the ups and downs of the relationship.

....

LESSON TWO

The purpose of this lesson is to help group members determine where they are in their marriage and would be a good time to create their second collage. Many women forget what their first collage looked like; when they made it, they were so numb. Directions for second collage:

1. Open back cover of their *Workbook* and unfold the flap.

2. Quickly close the first collage cover so that you don't have a chance to spend any time looking at the first collage yet.

3. Fold the second collage page back so that it is the only page exposed as you look at the back of the *Workbook*.

4. Create your second collage, using magazines to express with words and pictures how they feel about where they are today.

5. Once the women have finished the second collage, open the back cover to exposed both collages.

6. Have them compare the collages and personally evaluate where they are now.

7. Encourage group members to think about what they will be doing in the year ahead to continue to pursuing healing.

In Lesson 4, we will be asking the women to come back to this lesson and put the healthy self care steps in the outer circle of their target. The target has three circles. Within the inner circle they will put areas they have discovered from their FASTER Scale that are relapses for them. In the middle circle will be ways of thinking or behaviors that lead them into relapse, and the outer circle will contain the new behaviors they want to incorporate into their life to create a healthy new lifestyle.

It is important for the women to review their Safety Plan every few months; this lesson serves as a reminder of that. If their spouse has been agreeable to the plan, it is a good reminder for women that he is working to gain their trust.

We don't want to get into theological issues on grounds for divorce, so we tried to give a broad brushstroke on what the Bible says and help women know abuse is not to be tolerated. If abuse is going on, a better solution would be separation rather than divorce (again depending on the level of abuse). That is where a Christian counselor and/or pastor should be brought into the decision making process. There are anger management classes the husband can take and if that is an issue in the marriage, the classes could be part of the wife's Safety Plan. Remind women dealing with life and death abuse, they should call 911 and also start working on steps 4 and 5 of their Safety Plan. If separation is in the works, here is a great resource to recommend by Lee Raffel, *Should I Stay or Go?—How Controlled Separation Can Save Your Marriage*.

Working through the Safe People section is really important. It will help group members recognize any progress in their spouse as far as him becoming more safe and trustworthy. Another resource you can encourage the women to watch is Brené Brown's *The Anatomy of Trust* which powerfully helps them evaluate the trust level with their spouse. If you don't have time to show it in one of the following lessons, you can plan to use it in your final celebration time together. The link is: www.supersoul.tv/super-soul-sessions/the-anatomy-of-trust/

LESSON THREE

One purpose of this lesson is to help women see that the thing they want the most is one of the hardest things for the addict to give them; empathy. Without good attachment, learned in his formative years, it is one of the most difficult skills he will need to gain to move their relationship towards intimacy. If the husband is in a Pure Desire men's group, there is hope. He will begin to empathize with other men in the group and also learn from them. His group will challenge him in this area. It's important for her to give him grace as he is learning this important dance step. One of the things we will challenge her to do in this lesson (if she is ready) is to define what she needs to feel pursued. She will need to share that with her spouse.

As stated in Chapter 9, Lesson 1, this lesson may be difficult for those going through separation or divorce. It is crucial for them to see what health looks like, especially, if God has not called them to be single the rest of their life.

Chapter 9, Lesson 3 (page 248) of the *Betrayal & Beyond Journal* provides a place for them to choose ways they would feel pursued and select some ideas for date nights. These are important exercises, especially for women who scored high in TA (Trauma Abstinence). The exercises will help them find their voice and express their opinions and needs.

A discussion on healthy and unhealthy sex is really important for the women to express and to hear from others. If there are sexual violations as stated in Chapter 6, Lesson 2, have the women in the group support a member, outlining healthy boundaries that need to be established so violations will not continue. Some women have avoided sex during their entire marriage. If women express a reluctance to have sex, even when their spouse is making great strides in building trust, she needs to see that her anorexia in this area of her life is not normal or healthy. There may be sexual abuse issues in her past that are hindering her from enjoying a close intimate and sexual relationship with her spouse. Encourage any women who are struggling with this issue to get Christian counseling. This would be a great area of growth that she could list in her Outer Circle in her Three Circles in the next lesson. It would be important for her to commit to this before the group ends. Group members would commit to call her and find out she is doing in this area. For some women, there may actually be physical pain involved with intercourse. Encourage a woman dealing with this issue, to seek medical help and/ or a naturopath who can give her natural hormones and testosterone to help alleviate the pain.

Challenge women who are ready to grow in their sexual intimacy to review the Developing Intimacy Exercise provided in the appendix of the *Workbook* on page 298. She should ask her husband if he would like to schedule a time for the two of them to talk about it. Not all couples are at a healthy place of healing yet. Encourage those who aren't ready to, at some point, come back and do that exercise when they are at a healthier point in their marriage.

Talk through the Three Circles exercise for the next week. This is crucial for future accountability with their inner and middle circle. The outer circle will help women establish a plan for future health and self care.

Your next meeting is your last group meeting; plan a celebration. My suggestion is to have the celebration after next week because they will be doing their target, and the next lesson will encourage them to come up with a Couple's Safety Plan.

Your last meeting should be a celebration! These women have dealt with one of the most difficult things in their lives. You might want to plan a dessert or potluck time, as well as do one or more of the following suggestions as a way to bring closure to your group:

- Have each woman share what she discovered as she worked through the exercises, especially the legacy she desires to leave.

- Since it is important that these women have a plan for their next step of healing and that they find someone who will hold them accountable to follow through, ask them to share their "next steps." Healing is not a one-time venture; it is a lifelong process.

- You may want to have prayer over each woman in light of what she has shared.

- You might also want to end with a helium balloon ceremony. Write on helium balloons any hopes and dreams or what you have to let go of to trust God in regards to your hopes and dreams. Pray over them and release them to the Lord symbolically by letting go of the balloons (use balloons that are environmentally friendly).

LESSON FOUR

If this is your last meeting, make sure you have time to go over the important parts of this lesson. It is crucial that the women have a plan so that they continue in their healing journey.

If some had a hard time coming up with commitments for their outer circle, spend time as a group and brain storm. A number of women might be ready to commit going through the *Workbook* again together. Help them recall the difference in their collage exercise. Point out that if they go through the group again, it would change that collage even more. Many women are very numb and lack focus the first three months of group because they are in such pain. We have reports of women who decide to return to group that say they don't even remember what they wrote down those first three months, but when they repeat the group, they are thrilled by how far they have come.

Make sure there is time set aside to share their dreams for the future; how they want to finish their "dash"—their legacy. Make time to pray for each of them. If you have another group time for celebration, you may want to wait to do this prayer during that celebration time.

As stated previously, for your final celebration, you might want to pull up the video (www.supersoul. tv/super-soul-sessions/the-anatomy-of-trust/) of Brené Brown and watch it as a group—the women can take notes in their *Betrayal & Beyond Journal* with the acrostic BRAVING. This would be a fitting close—since we have called them to be brave heroines—this delineates what a brave heroine looks like. Here are the definitions of the acrostic she uses:

BRAVING

B - Boundaries

R - Reliability

A - Accountability

V - Vault

I - Integrity

N - Non-judgment

G - Generosity

FINAL CELEBRATION

- Plan ways to celebrate—perhaps a dessert or potluck.
- Go over homework from week four.
- You might also want to show the Brené Brown video—which is about 20 minutes long.
- Spend time praying over the dreams the women have.
- Challenge them to pick women in their group to hold them accountable for their next steps toward healing—especially the ones they put in their Third Circle.

Where do I go from here? Many women will want to turn around and help others through a Betrayal & Beyond group. Most of my leaders, who have repeated the group experience, acknowledge that there were more layers God healed when they repeated a Betrayal & Beyond group. Others, whose marriages are moving forward, might want to create couples' groups and go through the *Sexy Christians* book, *Workbook*, and DVD; the exercises in the book, *Workbook*, and DVD are in-depth and support what the women have been working through in Betrayal & Beyond. *Sexy Christians* was written to help couples create real intimacy in all areas—physical, emotional, and spiritual.

We would love to hear from you about your group experiences and any suggestions you have to improve the material. Any input or suggestions for you as a leader that we could add online would also be greatly appreciated. You can contact our Women's Groups Coordinator at ashleyj@puredesire.org.

❓ Do I have to have a church backing?

It's preferable to have support from your church's leadership team. That team can provide prayer support, can advertise the group to help you find group members, and can provide a safe, secure meeting space. However, if for some reason your church is not able to provide such support, you may be able to meet independent of your church if you are in contact with a Pure Desire support network. Either way, it is extremely important for a group leader herself to be supported by some form of mentorship, through her church and/or through Pure Desire Ministries.

❓ How can I get support through Pure Desire Ministries?

Contact our office at 503.489.0230 or info@puredesire.org and we can put you in contact with the group leadership team overseeing your area.

❓ Is it okay to meet in my home or a coffee shop instead of the church?

Safety, confidentiality and accessibility are the most important factors in choosing a meeting location. A public location, such as a restaurant or public park, is not ideal because it is not confidential. Whether you open your home to the group is personal choice; however, consider carefully whether you feel safe with this choice, whether your home is easily accessible, and whether you are able to provide a confidential location, free of interruptions, for the group meeting time. If you choose to host the group in your home, be aware that it is often more difficult to hold to the two-hour group time limit. Women tend to linger longer in a home than in a church facility.

❓ What if someone breaks confidentiality?

Breaking confidentiality makes the group feel unsafe and needs to be taken very seriously. The person who broke the group's confidentiality needs to be made aware of the seriousness of this, should attempt to make amends to the person they wronged, and will very likely need to leave the group.

❓ What are the guidelines on absences?

Group members must make these meetings a priority. While illness and emergencies do occur occasionally, if a group member misses three or more meetings it may not be the right time for them to be in a group. Absences not only interfere with their own ability to learn and apply the material, but those absences can make other group members feel unsafe about sharing their stories and unsettled about whether or not the absentee member is invested in the process. If a member cannot make it to group because of an emergency or illness, you may want to add to the Group Guidelines that they can contact another group member before the next meeting to catch up on the material covered.

❷ Can a new member join an existing group?

Some groups prefer to close their meetings after the first several lessons. Others, however, have 'open groups,' allowing new members to join at any time. The group leader will need to determine her preference, and to discuss her policy with the group members so that the policy is set at the beginning. As stated previously, open groups may accept new members up through Chapter 7.

❷ Does the group really have to be two hours long?

A two hour meeting block allows a group of four to six members ample time to form relationships, to check in, and to discuss the curriculum. If a group is smaller, a 90 minute group time may suffice. Groups larger than six or seven members are not recommended.

❷ Do we have to meet every week?

While there will be missed weeks due to holidays or other conflicts with calendars, maintaining consistency with meeting schedules is important.

❷ Do we have to contact each other throughout the week?

The short answer is 'yes.' Women may need support throughout the week as they go through the curriculum and experience reactions to some of that work. Additionally, women need to learn to lean on other safe women when they are tempted to relapse into codependent or reactive behavior, to be sure they are using their newly-learned tools, and to share successes throughout the week. Part of the beauty of this work is forming relationships with other women who understand.

❷ What if someone is not doing their homework?

If someone consistently comes without completing their homework, it may not be the right time for them to be in a group. The group leader should talk with them about why the work is not getting done, assess their level of commitment, and help them decide whether or not they are willing to complete that work. If not, they cannot continue in group as the other women will not feel safe sharing their own work.

❷ What if the women are facing very different life situations (engaged, married, separated, in the process of divorce or already divorced)? What about age differences?

While it's tempting to put all of the women who are facing the same issues together, we actually find it more helpful to cross-group the women. This way, women realize that every marriage is different, that they are all in different places, and they are able to gain support from each other's stories. If you have a large number of women you are assigning to groups and there are two single or divorced women, we recommend that you place them together so they can relate with someone going through a similar experience.

INTEGRATING NEW WOMEN
INTO AN EXISTING BETRAYAL & BEYOND GROUP

New women may join at the **beginning** of any chapter between Chapter 1 and Chapter 7.

However, we highly recommend that women complete an orientation session before joining an existing class. This orientation may include several women or may be one-on-one with a leader.

AN ORIENTATION SESSION INCLUDES:

1. Completion of the survey and questionnaire (optional)

2. Reading and signing the Memo of Understanding

3. Review of the Small Group Guidelines

4. Instructions about completing the lessons in Chapter 1, which provides some foundational information for understanding all the chapters.

Beyond the lessons in Chapter 1, it is not necessary for a woman to "catch up" by doing additional chapters to bring her to where an existing group is working. She will want to do those chapters as part of her healing, but should complete them during another group cycle.

In fact, many women will want to repeat the cycle of the nine chapters. As they move beyond betrayal and into deeper levels of healing, they will be ready to learn and understand things that they could not grasp during the first time through the chapters.

BETRAYAL & BEYOND SURVEY

Thank you for taking the time to fill out this confidential survey. Your openness will help us more fully understand your emotional and spiritual needs.

PLEASE PRINT

Name _____ Date _____

Address _____

City _____ Zip _____

Email _____

Home Phone _____ Cell _____ Work _____

Church Affiliation _____

Marital Status ☐ Single   ☐ Married   ☐ Separated   ☐ Divorced

Spouse's Name _____

Please list the names and ages of your children:

_____

_____

_____

Please list the names of any close friends or family also attending this Betrayal & Beyond group:

_____

➲ Please check all the issues/feelings you are presently experiencing or with which you have recently struggled.

➲ Of those you checked, circle the two most pressing concerns for you now.

☐ Depression

☐ Anxiety/Fear

☐ Anger

☐ Guilt/Shame

☐ Low Self-Esteem/Lack of Confidence

☐ Perfectionism or Obsessive Behavior

☐ Substance Abuse (alcohol, drugs)

☐ Eating Disorder or Weight Problems (anorexia, bulimia, binge eating or overeating)

☐ Addictions (other than those listed above, such as gambling, smoking, sex, work)

☐ Problems Obtaining or Keeping a Job

☐ Relationship Problems (marriage, dating, family, friends)

☐ Spousal Abuse/Violence

Note: Please bring this completed survey to the first group meeting or complete the survey before you leave the first group meeting. Return it to your group leader.

BETRAYAL & BEYOND QUESTIONNAIRE

1. The biggest problem I struggle with:

_____

_____

_____

_____

2. When I get angry with God, it's usually because:

_____

_____

_____

_____

3. Rate your Christian walk on a scale of 1-10 (10 being great). What area in your spiritual life causes you to sin or stumble the most?

1	2	3	4	5	6	7	8	9	10
Empty/Nothing				Okay					Great!

_____

_____

_____

_____

4. What do you hope to gain from this group?

_____

_____

_____

_____

5. On a scale of 1-10 (10 being most honest), how honest were you in answering these questions?

1	2	3	4	5	6	7	8	9	10
Not honest at all				Somewhat honest					Most honest

This questionnaire is intended to be anonymous.

RECOMMENDED READING

- Black, Claudia, Ph.D. *Deceived: Facing Sexual Betrayal, Lies, and Secrets*. City Center, MN: Hazelden, 2009.

- Carnes, Patrick. *Don't Call It Love*. New York: Bantam Books, 1991.

- Carnes, Patrick J., Ph.D. *The Betrayal Bond*. Deerfield Beach, FL: Health Communications, Inc., 1997.

- Carnes, Stephanie, ed. *Mending A Shattered Heart: A Guide for Partners of Sex Addicts*. AZ: Gentle Path Press, 2008.

- Cloud, Henry, & John Townsend. *Boundaries*. Grand Rapids: Zondervan, 1992.

- Cloud, Henry, & John Townsend. *Safe People*. Grand Rapids: Zondervan, 1995.

- Dye, Michael, CADC, NCAC II, *The Genesis Process for Change Groups*. Auburn, CA: Michael Dye, 2006. www.genesisprocess.org.

- Hall, Laurie. *An Affair of the Mind*. Colorado Springs: Focus on the Family Publishing, 1996.

- Kendall, RT. *Total Forgiveness*. Lake Mary, FL: Charisma House, 2002.

- McIlhaney, Joe S., MD, & Freda McKissic Bush, MD. *Hooked: New Science on How Casual Sex is Affecting Our Children*. Chicago: Northfield Publishing, 2008.

- Penner, Clifford & Joyce. *Restoring the Pleasure*. Dallas: Word Publishing, 1993.

- Roberts, Ted. *Pure Desire*. Ventura: Regal Books, 1999.

- Roberts, Ted. *Seven Pillars of Freedom Workbook, Journal, and Leader's Guide*. Gresham, OR: Pure Desire Ministries International, 2009. www.puredesire.org

- Spring, Janis A. *How Can I Forgive You? The Courage to Forgive, the Freedom Not To*. New York: Harper Collins, 2004.

- Steffens, Barbara, Ph.D. & Marsha Means, MA. *Your Sexually Addicted Spouse: How Partners Can Cope and Heal*. Far Hills: New Horizon Press, 2009.

- Weiss, Douglas, Ph.D. *Partners: Healing from His Addiction*. Colorado Springs: Discovery Press, 2001.

- Wilson, Meg. *Hope After Betrayal: Healing When Sexual Addiction Invades Your Marriage*. Grand Rapids: Kregel Publications, 2007.

WHEN YOU ARE READY FOR SEXUAL INTIMACY

As you rebuild trust with your spouse and are ready for sexual intimacy, one or both of you may experience some body responses that inhibit physical intimacy. As with other physical symptoms that seem abnormal, you may want to consult a physician for advice. The following books may also be helpful to your understanding of how betrayal may have impacted your ability to achieve sexual fulfillment.

- Roberts, Ted & Diane. *Sexy Christians*. Grand Rapids: Baker Books, 2010. Recommended after both husband and wife have completed their Pure Desire Curriculum—*Betrayal & Beyond* for her and the *Seven Pillars of Freedom* for him. www.puredesire.org.

- Dr. Sue Johnson, *Hold Me Tight*. New York: Little Brown and Co., 2009

- Patrick Carnes. *Sexual Anorexia: Overcoming Sexual Self-Hatred*. Center City, Minnesota: Hazelden, 1997.

- Clifford & Joyce Penner. *Restoring the Pleasure*. Nashville: Thomas Nelson, 1993.

- Douglas Weiss. *Sexual Anorexia: Beyond Sexual, Emotional and Spiritual*.

WHAT A POLYGRAPH TEST CAN AND CANNOT DO

The polygraph test is one tool that can be used to begin to restore trust in a relationship. It can be given within 30 days of disclosure or discovery and can be followed up every 90 days by another one to ensure greater accountability. If trust begins to grow, you may want to repeat the test every six months, and then go to one every year, depending upon the type of addiction.

Most sex addicts don't like the idea of a polygraph test because they have never had their behavior measured objectively. But over time, we have found that men who are serious about walking in health actually see this as a helpful measure of how they are moving towards health. Also, when they know there will be a follow-up test, it helps them to think twice about the temptation to fall back into old patterns.

The polygraph cannot guarantee that he will not lie again or that he will stop his addictive behavior, but it can promote safety and trust. Although this tool can begin to help reestablish trust, the goal is to leave the tool behind eventually and begin to trust based on a growing intimacy in the relationship.

CAUTION!

There are a few cautions we give to wives who have requested this test:

1. Be careful that the polygraph not be used to feed into the codependent need to be a detective.

2. If the husband passes, don't challenge the test. If you have concerns, wait until the next polygraph test. If there are inconsistencies in his behavior, expect them to be revealed in the next polygraph test.

FULL DISCLOSURE POLYGRAPH TESTS

The most effective polygraph tests are "full disclosure polygraphs" that take between two to three hours initially. We recommend you use a CSAT counselor (check under Counseling > Affiliate Treatment Providers on puredesire.org or call our office for a counselor). Many of the counselors listed can help you via video if you are not located near one we recommend. The addict will need to submit a detailed sexual history of his sexual behaviors as far back as he can remember up to present day. It will include all sexual behavior outside the marriage bed. The counselor will look it over to make sure nothing is left out. The addict takes his full sexual history and 3-5 questions from the wife to the polygraph examiner who will ask him questions in light of those two documents.

You can check the yellow pages under "polygraph," Google "polygraph examiner," or check with local attorneys who can put you in contact with someone who can give a "full disclosure polygraph." Our Pure Desire office also has polygraphers we can recommend and a written statement to the polygrapher that explains the purpose of the polygraph.

WHAT DO I DO WITH THE RESULTS?

It is best to have the results sent to a counselor who can debrief you as a couple.

QUESTIONS FOR THE POLYGRAPH TEST

The polygraph examiner will need 3-5 yes or no questions submitted by the wife in a sealed envelope. This allows the wife to have specific questions she might have, answered.

The following suggestions will help you write out your own personal questions that can be included in the polygraph. Because many women have no idea what to ask, we have provided some examples. The comments in parenthesis give you options with specific time frames: since we have been married, since we started counseling, since you joined a Pure Desire group.

Note: If you are asking questions about sex with minors, find out ahead of time if the examiner is a mandatory reporter. If he feels any children are at risk, he by law, in most cases, must report his findings, which can lead to criminal charges.

1. Have you had sexual contact with another woman during the course of our marriage? If so, have you had more than one? If so, do I know her? If so, do you still have contact with this person through a social or work environment or social media?

2. Have you gone looking or cruising where prostitutes hang out during the course of our marriage? Have you had sexual contact with a prostitute? Have you visited topless bars?

3. Have you paid for and received sexual favors from anyone, male or female, during the course of our marriage?

4. Have you ever had a physical or sexual relationship with another man? Have you ever had physical or sexual contact with a man more than once?

5. In the course of our marriage (or since we started Pure Desire groups/counseling) have you used the Internet with the intent to act out sexually? Have you used the TV to act out sexually? Have you used movies to act out sexually? Have you used the cell phone to act out sexually?

6. Have you used masturbation to meet your sexual needs during our marriage (or since we started counseling, or since you joined a Pure Desire group)? Have you used masturbation more than once a week to meet your sexual needs during the course of our marriage?

7. Have you been totally honest about all these issues with your wife? Have you been totally honest with your men's group that you are accountable to and/or your counselor?

8. As an adult have you had sexual contact with children? (**Caution! The answers in question eight could lead to criminal charges.**)

PTSI ANALYSIS OVERVIEW

© Copyright Patrick J. Carnes, PhD, CAS 1999

Based on your scores for the Post-Traumatic Stress Index (PTSI), the following is a brief explanation of what the score measures. If you have been in recovery then these are possible "vulnerable" areas of which to be aware.

- If your score is **low (0-2)**, this is not an area of concern.
- If your score is **moderate (3-6)**, you may wish to explore strategies that might help resolve the past or how to reduce your vulnerability in this area.
- If your score is **severe (7-18)**, then this is an area of potential intense focus for you or an area of periodic significance.

Obviously, the higher the number, the more concern one has about the severity and chronicity of brain change.

Please note that this screening instrument assists in beginning to think about the potential role of trauma or relational experiences in your life.

Further assessment with a therapist will determine if these results "fit" and what protocols to consider.

TRT - TRAUMA REACTIONS

Experiencing current reactions to trauma events in the past. This relates to post-traumatic stress disorder (PTSD) symptoms and a tendency to over-react or under-react. Most individuals who score in this area experienced some kind of anxiety (stress) in their family of origin, or growing up and feeling a sense of fear or terror (lack of safety). This sense of uncertainty may be acute or chronic and longitudinal. The general idea is that perceived trauma by an individual results in the release of stress hormones, which may actually damage (rewire) the brain when stress is sustained.

TYPICAL THERAPEUTIC STRATEGIES:

- Study and write down your automatic "knee jerk" reactions and distorted thinking.
- Write letters to those who facilitated less-than nurturing experiences for you, telling them of the long-term impact you are experiencing.
- Also write amends letters to those you know you have harmed.
- Decide with a therapist what is appropriate to send.
- You may need to wait until you are further along in your individual and coupleship (if applicable) recovery before attending to amends.

TR - TRAUMA REPETITION

Repeating behaviors or situations that parallel early relationally traumatic experiences. This relates to reenactment and the tendency to "do over." Individuals who score in this area often report OCD or OCPD features (hyper-focus, obsession, rumination).

TYPICAL THERAPEUTIC STRATEGIES:

- Understand how history repeats itself in your life experiences.
- Develop habits which help to center yourself (e.g., breathing, journaling, meditation, light exer-

cise) so you are doing what you intend -- not the cycles of old.

- Work on boundaries, both external and internal. Boundary failure is key to repetition compulsion.

TBD - TRAUMA BONDS

Being connected (loyal, helpful or supportive) to people who are dangerous, shaming or exploitative. People who score in this area tend to trust those they should not and to mistrust those they should.

TYPICAL THERAPEUTIC STRATEGIES:

- Learn to recognize trauma bonds by identifying those in your life.
- Look for patterns.
- Use "detachment" strategies in difficult situations or with people who "trigger" your codependence.

TS - TRAUMA SHAME

Feeling unworthy, or helpless/hopeless/worthless; having self-hate because of trauma experience. This relates to a sense of self, self-esteem and the experience of thinking "I'm not enough" and "I'm not safe" (e.g., "I can't be myself and be enough, and I'm not safe in this world... being who I am"). Often, individuals will react to stress with extremes (underfunctioning or overfunctioning, grandiosity or worthlessness, over-control or helplessness and avoidance or passive-aggressive behavior, excessive neediness or hopelessness).

TYPICAL THERAPEUTIC STRATEGIES:

- Understand shame dynamics in your family of origin and how those patterns repeat in your relationships today.
- To whom was it important that you feel ashamed?
- Write a list of your secrets.
- Begin reprogramming yourself with 10 affirmations, 10 times a day (in front of the mirror is best).

TP - TRAUMA PLEASURE NEUROPATHWAY

This is one of the addictive neuropathways related to intensity. When the brain is triggered limbically, automatic reactions ensue and defenses (familiar coping mechanisms) result. Individuals who score in this area often find pleasure in the presence of extreme danger, violence, risk or shame. Thoughts/behaviors primarily used to reduce pain and acted out with Intensity, Risk, Danger, Power/Control.

TYPICAL THERAPEUTIC STRATEGIES:

- Write a history of how excitement and shame are linked to your trauma past.
- Note the costs and dangers to you over time.
- Write a First Step and relapse prevention plan about how powerful this is in your life.

HOW THIS NEUROPATHWAY FACILITATES BEHAVIORAL SYMPTOMS IN VARIOUS AREAS:

1. Erotic (sexual): All focus is on erotic behavior, excitement, sexual possibility and orgasm. High intensity, risk and danger are often associated. Trauma survivors may incorporate pain and trauma into behavior. Violent/Painful S&M. Voyeuristic Rape. Humiliation. Degradation. Anonymous. Prostitutes. One-night stands. Exhibitionism. Swinging/Swapping. Massage Parlors. Adult Bookstores. Frotterism. Masturbation w/or without porn or 900#.

2. Romance (sexual): Romance junkies turn new love into a "fix." They fall into love repeatedly or simultaneously. Roller-coaster romances are highly sexual, volatile, and dangerous. Partners are often unreachable, unavailable or unreadable. Seduction. Exploitation. Conquest. Flirtation. Fatal Attraction syndrome. Having sex with employees and professional "relationships." Office romances. Affair with neighbor. Affairs. Harassment. Swinging/Swapping. Clubs/Bars.

3. Relationship (sexual): Volatile, intense, controlling and often dangerous relationships. Traumatic bonding, stalking and codependency thrive in abandonment, fear-based or dangerous collaborations. Cycles of sex and breakups. High involvement with a stalker. Keep trying to "break it off." Seen in public with a lover. Domestic Violence Syndrome.

4. Drugs/Money/Food: Methamphetamine, Cocaine, Ecstasy, Violence. Craps, Race Track. Over-eating. When facilitated in Health (ability to self-soothe): Life-Enhancing, Passion, Advocacy.

TB - TRAUMA BLOCKING NEUROPATHWAY

This is one of the addictive neuropathways related to numbing. When the brain is triggered limbically, automatic reactions ensue and defenses (familiar coping mechanisms) result. Patterns exist to numb and block out overwhelming feelings that stem from trauma in your life. The unconscious need is for satiation and trancing, which is used to soothe the anxiety and stress of daily life. Behavior is used to sleep, to calm down, or to manage internal discomfort. Anxiety occurs when highly ritualized behavior is frustrated or disturbed. Thoughts/Behaviors primarily used to reduce anxiety.

TYPICAL THERAPEUTIC STRATEGIES:

- Work to identify experiences in which you felt pain or diminished.
- Re-experience the feelings in a safe place with the help of your therapist and make sense of them as an adult. This will reduce the power they have had in your life.
- Write a First Step if necessary.

HOW THIS NEUROPATHWAY FACILITATES BEHAVIORAL SYMPTOMS IN VARIOUS AREAS:

1. Erotic (sexual): Sex is used to soothe the anxiety and stress of daily life. Sex is used to sleep, to calm down high-risk takers, or to manage internal discomfort. Anxiety occurs when highly ritualized behavior is frustrated or disturbed. Masturbation to sleep. Adult Bookstores. Lounges. 900#. Internet. Voyeurism.

2. Romantic (sexual): Romance becomes a way to manage anxiety. Person becomes anxious if not in love with someone or with the person loved. How you are and who the other is not as important as the comfort of being attached. The only goal is to be with someone. Avoid being alone/lonely at all costs. Serial or simultaneous dating/ marriage. CoSA/S-Anon.

3. Relationship (sexual): Compulsive relationships include tolerating the intolerable – battering, addiction, abuse and deprivation. Person will distort reality rather than face abandonment. Domestic Violence.

4. Drugs/Money/Food: Alcohol, Valium, Heroin. Slot Machines. Over-eating. When facilitated in Health (ability to self-soothe): Reflective, Calming, Solitude.

TSG - TRAUMA SPLITTING NEUROPATHWAY

This is one of the addictive neuropathways related to dissociation. Dissociation exists on a continuum from "simply spacing out sometimes when driving" to severe Dissociative Identity Disorder. When the brain is triggered limbically, automatic reactions ensue and defenses (familiar coping mechanisms) result. Ignoring traumatic realities by dissociating or compartmentalizing experiences or parts of the self. Flighting in to fantasy and unreality as an escape. Dissociation and OCD symptoms are typical. Obsession and preoccupation become the solution to painful reality. Fantasy is an escape used to procrastinate, avoid grief and ignore pain. The neurochemicals involved are typically estrogens and androgens that occur naturally for libido, lust and the drive to procreate. In terms of courtship disorder, this results in dysfunctional patterns of noticing, attraction, touching and foreplay. Thoughts/behaviors primarily used to reduce shame. Acting out with Dissociation, Compartmentalizing, Escape, Obsession.

TYPICAL THERAPEUTIC STRATEGIES:

- Learn that dissociating is a "normal" response to trauma.

- Identify ways you split reality and the triggers that cause that to happen.

- Cultivate a "caring" adult who stays present so you can remain whole.

- Notice any powerlessness you feel and how you're drawn to control or having to know exactly what/how/why, or managing the outcome, and may experience difficulty with flexibility and trusting the process.

HOW THIS NEUROPATHWAY FACILITATES BEHAVIORAL SYMPTOMS IN VARIOUS AREAS:

1. Erotic (sexual): Obsession and preoccupation become the solution to painful reality. Fantasy is an escape used to procrastinate, avoid grief and ignore pain. Ultimate orgasm, Strip clubs. Swinging/Swapping. Cruising. Cybersex. Porn. 900#. High ritualization.

2. Romantic (sexual): Person avoids life problems through romantic preoccupation. Planning, intrigue and research fill the void. Emails and chats, magical romance and stalking are more real than family. Erotic Stories. Sexual misconduct. Stalking. Internet "soulmate."

3. Relationship (sexual): Compulsive relationships are built on distorted fantasy. Charisma, role, cause, gratitude play role in cults, sexual misconduct and betrayal. Mystique is built on secrecy, belief in uniqueness, and "special" needs/wants. "Cosmic Relationship."

4. Drugs/Money/Food: Cannabis, LSD. Internet Lottery. Binge-Purge. When facilitated in Health (ability to self-soothe): Focus(ed).

TA - TRAUMA ABSTINENCE

As a result of traumatic experience, individuals who score in this area tend to deprive (also noted as Trauma Deprivation or TD) themselves of things that are wanted, needed or deserved. There is difficulty in meeting for, or asking for help in meeting, one's needs and wants. Trauma Aversion is used to reduce terror/fear by providing a false sense of control. Often individuals will experience or act out in extremes or binge/purge patterns. Thoughts/Behaviors used primarily to reduce terror/fear. Acted out with Control and Binge-Purge.

TYPICAL THERAPEUTIC STRATEGIES:

- Understand how deprivation is a way to continue serving your perpetrators.

- Write a letter to the victim that was you in the past and how you learned to tolerate pain and deprivation.

- Work on strategies to self-nurture and protect/comfort your inner child.

- Visualize yourself as a precious child of the universe.

HOW THIS NEUROPATHWAY FACILITATES BEHAVIORAL SYMPTOMS IN VARIOUS AREAS:

1. Erotic (sexual): Anything erotic or suggestive is rejected. Sex is threatening, mundane, tolerable; not pleasurable. Sex may be okay if the other person does not matter (objectified). Self-mutilation. Objectification of self, being used (prostitution).

2. Romantic (sexual): Extreme distrust of romantic feelings or initiatives. At best person seeks "arrangement." Marriage without sex. Suspicious of kindness (seeks ulterior motives). Avoid and withdraw.

3. Relationship (sexual): Avoids. Isolated, lonely, restricted emotions and poor or nonexistent communication skills. May be overly intellectual/analytical. Secret attachments (nobody can know that I care about…)

4. Drugs/Money/Food: Under-earning, Hoarding. When facilitated in Health (ability to self-soothe): Ascetic (for a higher purpose – as in choosing celibacy as a spiritual way of life, or abstinence for a specific period of time to promote self-awareness and healthy nurturing).

SAMPLE BETRAYAL & BEYOND LETTER BY LISA STAMBAUGH

Dear Sister,

Receiving this letter indicates that you have a loved one who is caught up in sexual bondage and is in the beginning stages of finding help. While we are encouraged that he is stepping out to get knowledge, healing, and support, we know this often means a woman is left behind who is desperate for answers, desperate for truth, and desperate for hope. We want you to know there are answers, there is truth, and there is hope for you.

Women initially feel very betrayed, angry, numb, and confused. While they may have known something was wrong, they didn't know exactly what it was. Even if confronted, he probably blamed her, turning the conversation back to her. If she did seek to get help specifically about his issues, she may have even been told that "men will be men," or that, somehow, the problem wouldn't be like it is if she was different in some way. These are lies that only prolong the issues and exacerbate her shame, paving the way for emotional catastrophes in her life.

The bottom line is that whether or not your husband chooses to become well, you can find healing and move forward. You do not need to continue in an emotional state of confusion, isolation, and pain. In fact, we have found that true restoration for marriages/relationships can only happen when both people choose to pursue their own healing.

One of the most helpful steps you can take is to complete the Betrayal and Beyond class for women affected by a loved one's sexual bondage. This class will give you the knowledge to grasp how sexual bondage is strangling your loved one, as well as the tools you need to move forward. We will help you identify vulnerabilities in your own life, so that you can guard against further harm and plan instead for a healthy future.

Listen to this testimony from one who went through this class in Gresham, Oregon:

"I came to Gresham from Montana just to attend the Betrayal & Beyond class. I felt swallowed up in darkness – the blackness that engulfed the man who had showed me a loving God, who was my friend and my marriage partner for twenty-four years. I was confused by the messages in my head and my heart. I was afraid of love, yet longed for its warm embrace. I was overwhelmed with guilt, sorrow, and shame.

In the class, I began to learn how to take care of myself. By listening and sharing in small group, I found that I wasn't crazy or alone! The fog of confusion began to lift as I learned what sexual addiction was and why it had destroyed the man I loved… A new depth of healing began, as I faced looking at myself in the mirror of truth. I had to take responsibility for the lies I believed, my codependency, and the anger and unforgiveness in my heart. I had to grieve all that had been lost. Then I was able to begin to set healthy boundaries to protect my heart and mind.

I have received great healing through this class and I know that I am God's loved and treasured daughter, held in the palm of His hands."

We hope you will join us in this journey of healing. You do not need to bear this burden alone. You can call [contact name] at this confidential number to find out more about the class: [phone number].

Sincerely,

[Pastor or Leader's Name]
[Church Name]

WIFE'S INVENTORY FOR DISCLOSURE [12]

A leader's resource to help those women who are going through a full disclosure

If a woman from your group wants to use this list, it is recommended that she do so with a sexual addiction therapist while going through the disclosure process.

❓ What are you hoping to receive by hearing your husband's disclosure?

⟳ Here is a general list that you can use to help you identify what you need to know in a disclosure. Mark the statements that would help you move toward healing.

1. A list of general addictive behaviors he has been involved in.

2. A list of specific addictive behaviors (share the amount of detail you want or specific information you need.

3. What are the time frames of these behaviors?

    A. Frequency and duration listed

4. Has your behavior involved another person/people?

    A. How many other partners were there?

    B. Were any partners male?

    C. What were the places/locations of the encounters?

    D. Do I know any of the people you were sexually involved with?

5. What information would you rather not know?

FURTHER QUESTIONS FOR YOU TO CONSIDER:

1. The need for a full history polygraph is explained in the appendix and recommended if he has consistently lied and had extramarital sex. This should be given before the above disclosure takes place.

2. Also consider if there anything you could hear in the disclosure that would cause you to want to leave the relationship. What is the deal breaker?

3. Do you have secrets you need to disclose to your husband in this process?

4. Do you have support and a self care plan for the day of disclosure.

5. What are your fears of going through a full disclosure?

---

12. 2008 Staci Sprout, LICSW, CSAT, more info at www.stacisprout.com

THE KARPMAN TRIANGLE EXERCISE

The Karpman Triangle, also known as the Drama Triangle, was developed by psychiatrist Steven Karpman in the 1970s. The following exercise can help the women better understand the Karpman Triangle dynamic as they look at their reactions in relationship and can also help them understand how to get off the triangle and into a more healthy communication flow.

YOU WILL NEED:

- Three chairs

- Three pieces of paper labeled "Rescuer," "Persecutor," and "Victim"

- Two volunteers from your group

- One situation (an argument or regrettable incident that may have occurred for one of the women, or one that you as group facilitator are willing to discuss) to process

PROCESS:

- Brief the group on the argument or regrettable incident to be processed.

- Form the three chairs into a triangle. Place one sign on each chair, as on the points of the Karpman Triangle.

- Process through the incident. As the situation unfolds, stop often and ask the women what role they are playing in that moment. The women should move to the different chairs as they realize when they are playing the role of Victim, Persecutor, or Rescuer.

EXAMPLE:

Situation: A teenage daughter has bad grades and will miss prom because of it.

Role Play: One woman plays the mother and one woman plays the teenager.

Exercise: The teenager may start in the Victim chair, as she feels she shouldn't have to miss prom because of her grades. The mom may sit in the Rescuer chair as she tries to contact the teachers to get extra credit assignments for her daughter to bring up her grades. However, as the mom sees the daughter not completing those extra credit assignments, she may switch over to the Persecutor chair and start yelling at the daughter for her lack of work ethic. The mom may then switch to the Victim chair as she continues to tell the daughter how hard she works and how she is not appreciated by the daughter for all she does. The daughter now moves to the Rescuer chair, saying she is going to do better,really does appreciate mom, and wants to show her how much, so she takes out the trash for her or buys her flowers…and it can go on and on as the women switch chairs as the role play continues for as long as is helpful.

After the exercise is completed, you may want to discuss how to get off the Karpman Triangle by using a healthy communication flow, consisting of Conversation, Communication and Compromise. Conversation begins the Communication process. Each side will likely need to make Compromises in order for both parties to feel safe in continuing the Communication flow. In healthy Communication, both participants take responsibility for what they think, say, and do. Neither feels the need to rescue or persecute the other and, as they are each identifying and communicating their needs, no one is a victim. You can think of healthy communication as a circle where both parties are equal, as opposed to the triangular form of the Karpman Triangle, which always puts one person at the less powerful, bottom apex of the triangle.